Making Schools Work

Making Schools Work

A Reporter's Journey Through
Some of America's
Most Remarkable Classrooms

Robert Benjamin

CONTINUUM · New York

ACKNOWLEDGMENTS

As a reporter, I am indebted first to the hundreds of students, parents and educators who shared their thoughts and time, as well as to the principals of schools across the country who opened their classroom doors.

Appreciation for financial support is due to the Ford Foundation, the Institute for Educational Leadership at George Washington University and *The Cincinnati Post*, where portions of this book originally appeared. In particular, acknowledgment should go to William R. Burleigh, editor of *The Post*, and to Michael Phillips, who was an assistant editor at the inception of this project.

Lynn Marmer Benjamin, my wife, provided wise counsel and patience. Her contributions to this book are beyond measure.

The author gratefully acknowledges the following for permission to use material: the Board of Education of the City of Chicago for the Chicago Mastery Learning Reading program © 1979 by the Board of Education of the City of Chicago; *Educational Leadership* magazine for "Mastery Learning Stifles Individuality" by Carl D. Glickman © 1979 by the Association for Supervision and Curriculum Development; SIMON & SCHUSTER, Inc., a division of the Gulf & Western Corporation, for *Your Child Can Succeed* by Siegfried Engelmann © 1975 by SIMON & SCHUSTER, Inc.; Phi Delta Kappa Educational Foundation for *The Restoration of Standards* by James C. Enochs © 1979 by the Phi Delta Kappa Educational Foundation; *Phi Delta Kappa* magazine for "Can Our Schools Get Better?" by John Goodlad © 1979 by *Phi Delta Kappa*.

1981
The Continuum Publishing Corporation
18 East 41st Street, New York, N.Y. 10017

Printed in the United States of America.

Library of Congress Cataloging in Publication Data

Benjamin, Robert.   Making schools work.
1.   Education, Urban—United States.
2.   Education, Elementary—United States.   I.   Title.
LC5131.B46   370.19′348′0973   80-26800   ISBN 0-8264-0040-X

In a social and political sense, it is a *Free* school system. It knows no distinction of rich and poor, of bond and free, or between those who, in the imperfect light of this world, are seeking, through different avenues, to reach the gate of heaven.

Horace Mann, 1848
Twelfth Annual Report from the secretary of the Massachusetts State Board of Education.

Contents

Introduction: *A Search*   1

1 / The Basics: *Beasley Academic Center*   11

2 / All Kids Can Learn: *Mastery Learning*   37

3 / The Politics of Reading: *DISTAR*   69

4 / The Principal Is The Key: *Garrison School*   100

5 / Case White A Revisited: *Edison School*   124

6 / The Limits of Human Relations: *Byck School*   146

7 / The Fourth R—Responsibility: *The Modesto Plan*   173

Introduction:
A Search

This book describes a search, a journey through some of urban America's most remarkable classrooms. It is about a rare set of elementary schools in which the children of the urban poor are learning.

The quest was hopeful: What makes schools work well? But it was set against a discouraging backdrop: the persistent failure of this nation's public schools to educate low-income students by even minimal standards.

It was a reporter's journey, rather than a professional educator's. It was undertaken with the belief that the benefits of this viewpoint outweigh its limitations, that all of us have a clear stake in shaping the solutions to what may prove to be the most challenging problem facing America's cities in the 1980s.

Its purpose was to demystify the elusive issue of how to create effective schools by pinpointing the building blocks of those that are already successful. If a certain educational philosophy emerges—one with social and political implications—the reader should be assured that it was developed empirically: by sitting in classrooms across the country.

The seeds of this journey were planted in similar fashion,

while observing students and teachers interacting in the classrooms of a large Midwestern city. The challenge then was to go beyond the surface politics of a desegregation battle to gauge the tenor of race relations among the city's children. Although race proved to be a pervasive issue among students, teachers, and parents, the truly rigid barriers were drawn along the lines of social class.

The city's public school system essentially was divided into two tiers: one for the middle class and one for the poor. Middle-income parents, who had had a strong hand in fostering this division, were of course acutely conscious of its effects. They didn't mind so much their children going to school with those of a different color; it was the children of the poor who were to be avoided.

And so, more affluent parents were possessive of their neighborhood schools and loathed sending their children "down the hill" to classes, while the less affluent used a variety of means to dodge their failing neighborhood schools. "Income," one parent observed, "is quickly becoming more important than race in the schools. For a long time, white people thought they were fighting a separate battle than black people. Now many white people are discovering *their* Johnnys can't read so well either."

Nothing drove home this educational fact of life more clearly than a map showing the relationship between students' reading achievement test scores and areas of poverty in the city. All the stars—for the elementary schools with the highest reading achievement—were positioned on the city's suburban fringes; all the blocks—for the elementary schools with the lowest reading achievement—sat squarely in the urban core or other pockets of poverty, both black and white.

A map like that can be drawn just as easily in almost every other urban school district in the country. Compare the average reading achievement test scores at schools in your area with the average income of students' families; more than likely, the two go hand in hand.

Most students—irrespective of their backgrounds— complete the first grade at roughly the same average achievement level, a largely unrecognized phenomenon. After that, however, low-income students tend to fall further behind their middle-class peers with each passing school year. By the sixth grade, the achievement gap between the two groups of children is as wide as four grade levels. As one inner-city mother of three described it: "You hardly ever see a kid in the first grade who isn't enthused. But by six months, the lights in their eyes are starting to go out. And soon, they just can't do any of the work."

Horace Mann, the father of American public education, viewed the public schools "beyond all other devices of human origin [as] the great equalizer of the conditions of men, the balance wheel of the social machinery." But Mann's dream remains unfulfilled, his "balance wheel" mired in the virtual lockstep correlation between social class and school success.

Contrary to a surprisingly resilient myth of equality, America's public schools typically do not equip the children of the poor for anything more than a second-class role in this country's society. The failure is systematic. Educators like nothing better than to point to singular examples of poor kids who've made it, but the public schools most everywhere amplify—more often than they mollify—the economic and social inequities of American life.

Indeed, the most extensive examination of student achievement ever conducted in this country, James Coleman's 1966 *Equality of Educational Opportunity* survey, concluded: ". . . the inequities imposed on children by their home, neighborhood and peer environment are carried along to become the inequities with which they confront adult life at the end of school. For equality of educational opportunity must imply a strong effect of schools that is independent of the child's immediate social environment, and that strong independent effect is not present in American schools."

So great is the achievement gap between low-income and middle-class students that *Giving Youth A Better Chance,* a 1979 report on youth and the schools by the Carnegie Council on Policy Studies in Higher Education, warned that "one-third of our youth are ill-educated, ill-employed, ill-equipped to make their way in American society. . . . As the already advantaged advance, the less advantaged tend to fall farther behind; and social cleavage widens and social unrest accelerates. We are in danger of developing a permanent underclass, a self-perpetuating culture of poverty, a substantial and continuing 'lumpen proletariat' in the 'home of opportunity where every man is the equal of every other man.' "

* * *

The sharp conclusions of the Coleman and Carnegie reports as to the relative impotence of public schooling in the face of poverty are underscored by the mixed record of most of the compensatory education efforts launched by urban districts and the federal and state governments in the 1960s and 1970s. The overriding lesson has been that merely providing additional resources is not the answer. And so at the beginning of the 1980s, the educational problems posed by low-income students seem more resistant to change in the public mind.

But the need for solutions only has increased. The flight of middle-class families from urban public schools continues, even as the energy and housing shortages promise to slow the thirty-year exodus from the urban centers. Most urban public school systems are growing smaller but face a higher percentage of low-income students with each new school year. By the end of the 1970s, students from poverty-level families made up more than 30 percent of the enrollments of many urban school districts.

Because of housing patterns and racial and social-class segregation within school systems, children from impoverished backgrounds usually are concentrated to an even greater degree in their classrooms—beyond a saturation point where the conventional ways of public schooling simply are addled. Theirs are schools in name only, serving the primary purpose of keeping them off the street. Research in six Midwestern cities in 1977 by Daniel Levine, of the University of Missouri at Kansas City, suggests there is a "threshold point" of about 40 percent low-income students "beyond which the schools as presently organized are unable to function effectively." The likely advent of vouchers—tax-supported plans to provide choices among schools, such as that already proposed in California—heralds even greater concentrations of low-income students, a future in which the public schools are abandoned to those least able to get out.

There are two common explanations for why schools usually don't make much of a difference in the lives of low-income children.

The most prevalent view places the blame on the students themselves, pointing to their family and social environments or their supposed limited abilities. This view—often espoused by educators—excuses school systems and their personnel from responsibility. "To understand our [low] test scores, you have to understand one-third of our kids are on welfare," explains the school superintendent, in one of the more typical versions of this argument.

The second view blames the system of American public education itself, pointing to the middle-class values embodied by educators and to this country's deeply ingrained racism and classism. This view simply dismisses any hope that public education can do much for those who are most dependent on it. "It's just like the welfare system," says the father of four who has watched his kids' minds wither as they've progressed through the schools in his inner-city neighborhood. "They come like beggars to the schools, and they end up with crumbs. The people working [in the schools] say, 'These kids can't learn and it's not my fault if they don't.' And parents are powerless in the face of it."

The bounds of these arguments are usually just that narrow as they clash in the schools of this nation's cities. It's a frustrating standoff between blame the victim and blame the system. Unfortunately, neither view offers much by way of solutions. What holds decided promise, instead, is the growing appreciation that some public schools—with the same concentrations of low-income children and the same resources—do a far better job than others by standard measures.

Some schools are thriving in bold contrast to the educational and emotional malaise evident in most schools in low-income areas. Educational researchers, who by and large did not formally recognize the potential importance of these successful, low-income schools until the 1970s, have come to call them "maverick schools" or "outliers"—for they are statistical standouts.

Given the overwhelmingly dismal achievement pattern of low-income students across the country, these maverick schools are appallingly rare. Ferreting them out, in the words of one researcher, can be "a treacherous enterprise." Increasingly conscious of their declining image, educators overly tout their would-be successes more often than not. And so a skeptical eye for the difference between what looks good on paper and what actually is occurring is necessary. In contrast to the public relations efforts, some mavericks apparently are kept from the public's view by intention. For instance, economist Thomas Sowell has noted a large, predominantly black metropolitan school on the West Coast "whose outstanding performance is kept quiet for fear of citizen demands to know why the other black schools in the same city cannot produce similar results."

Most public school systems, indeed, have reason to be threatened by the existence of maverick schools. For the observer willing to be open-minded about what leads to measurable results, examining these schools holds the promise of finding out what makes a positive difference in the lives of low-income children—to say nothing of how most of their schools are not serving them.

On this score, some researchers and educators are so heartened by the solutions already suggested by these few effective schools that they dare to predict that public education will strike an upbeat note in the 1980s. "I see a lot of understandings beginning to come together for the first time in the foreseeable future," said Lawrence Lezotte, an educational psychologist at Michigan State University. "In the '80s, the struggle for equal educational opportunity will give way to the goal of equal educational outcomes. It's inevitable that we won't be satisfied with equal access and will begin to talk about equal outcomes in the fullest sense.

"The question of effective schools for low-income students is at the heart of the whole question of the role of the schools in a democratic society. The long-run survival of democracy depends not so much on how the top fares as bridging the gap between the top and bottom. There's going to be a major initiative toward this; it's likely to become an issue in political campaigns. Just like we were once promised 'A chicken in every pot' or 'Two cars in every garage,' you'll hear 'We can teach everyone to read.' "

* * *

This journey began as a search for maverick schools. Put simply, I was looking for the best schools in some of the worst areas of the country. My goal was to spend as much time as possible in their classrooms and with their students, teachers, administrators, and parents. The approach was qualitative, particularly in contrast to the more traditional research method of attempting to isolate relatively narrow educational factors.

The field of search was limited to elementary schools for two reasons. The first was the assumption that there is more agreement about educational goals at the lower grade levels; imparting mastery of basic reading skills, it can be argued, makes up at least three-quarters of the task of elementary schools. The second assumption involved the obviously critical nature of this level of schooling; most of the problems at urban junior and senior highs inevitably can be traced back to failure at the elementary level. As one elementary school principal put it: "If you send kids to junior high who can read and write well, I don't care too much what you do with them later on—they'll do well. And if they can't read or write well, the ballgame is over."

My initial and rough measuring stick was to look for non-selective elementary schools where at least 60 percent of the children were eligible for free lunches (a convenient criterion for judging income) and where there was a history of at least half of the sixth graders reading at or above their grade level according to standardized achievement tests (the national norm). Reliance on these tests by itself can be criticized as too narrow, and perhaps rightfully so. However, in taking a national view of a decidedly local enterprise, it is the only solid signpost available; America's

$130-billion public education industry has not made it easy
for the public to measure the effectiveness of its delivery of
services. Quite often nationally normed tests are proclaimed as valid instruments, standard measures, when the
figures look good. When the numbers indicate failure, however, they often are dismissed as irrelevant or invalid. It
then is worth noting again that so few urban schools with
high concentrations of low-income students succeed by this
standard that they truly make up a select collection of
schools.

The search went astray often, sometimes as the result of
forthright tips offered by previous researchers. There were
schools that selectively skim off the very top students from a
low-income area or an entire school district—essentially a
rigged situation. There were schools that had only begun to
show improvement, however great. Some schools had many
low-income children who were faring poorly but also substantial numbers of high-income students who were pushing the schools' average achievement records to decep-
tively high levels. And there were schools that apparently
had once been models but were no longer working so well.
Along the way, though, there were some rather noteworthy
schools, true mavericks.

Each of them—true mavericks or not—proved to be a
separate world with its own particular lessons, a community
within larger communities. And these lessons are as much
about how to make schools work as how to observe,
evaluate, make sense out of what's going on in the first
place. Although these schools primarily serve low-income
students, there is little reason to believe their lessons could
not apply to middle-class schools. Few schools could not
stand improvement.

The solutions these schools suggest are not academic, but
pragmatic; they are not perfect models, only examples of

schools that are more or less effective at common, important tasks. In that sense, there can be no claim that this journey is complete, and the reader is urged to continue the search in his own way with his own eyes, perhaps better armed. The descriptions of schools in this book are offered with just that in mind. Use them.

1

The Basics:
Beasley Academic Center

No time for talking, not a moment to spare. A new school day is dawning at the Beasley Academic Center, and Maggie Brown Thomas's third graders silently stream in, ready to work.

They take their appointed seats in Room 229 with businesslike dispatch and attentive postures. No one is chewing gum or wearing jeans. Everyone has their books, their pencils, their homework. "How did you do on those interrogative and declarative sentences?" one of the eight-year-olds whispers to another, as last night's assignment—two hours of old-fashioned grammar—emerges from dog-eared folders for grading.

No one's at the pencil sharpener. The school's intercom is quiet; its corridors are clear. A sense of organized urgency pervades the air.

The nuts and bolts of reading are all around. A large phonics chart displaying the different sounds that make up words dominates a side wall. Paragraph and sentence drills fill the front blackboard; more exercises line the board in the back. Atop each desk are a blank piece of paper, a worksheet on prefixes, and a book that teaches the skill of discerning the main idea from reading passages.

After 30 seconds of directions, each of the 32 black children turns to attacking the morning's tasks. It's 9:07, and everyone knows what to do, what's expected.

"The first thing is you can't waste any time at all," explains Mrs. Thomas, a tall, thin black woman so strong-minded about the way children should be taught she'd send shivers up the spines of most of her colleagues across the country. "You don't want to leave time for talking, time for anything. If there's nothing on the boards or on their desks for them to do when they walk in, that's just lost time. Kids can't start by themselves. The average child likes the teacher to be organized. The average child works because something's expected, because there's a goal. I set goals for these kids, and I tell them what I expect of them."

A minute's walk away across State Street—deep in the heart of Chicago's south side—day breaks, too, for the teen-agers huddling in the graffiti-marked vestibules beneath the 28 sixteen-story towers in the world's largest housing project. But dawn at the Robert Taylor Homes portends only another round of dim expectations and thwarted goals, another day of second-class chances at the bottom of the city's social order.

Built in 1962 by the Chicago Housing Authority, the "Homes" is a $100-million monstrosity. The identical, massive, prisonlike buildings are monuments to misery, a nightmare of public planning well deserving their local epithet, "the world's largest mistake." It's a super-ghetto, two miles of concrete sandwiched between South State and the Dan Ryan Expressway. State Street, as a local writer once put it, is "no great street" in this part of town.

Twice as many people live in the overheated brick towers as did in the 95 acres of slums they replaced. More than 20,000 people—virtually all black, nine out of ten receiving some form of public assistance—are stockpiled here in about 4000 apartments spaced along outdoor hallways screened in by wire mesh from top to bottom. More than two-thirds of them are children.

The children of the Homes know to keep one eye to the sky, out of fear of being hit by an object tossed from one of the overhead walkways. They know about western-style shootouts and the dangers that lurk in the stairwells. "We see everything," says a 10-year-old. "The teenagers be shooting bullets from building to building for the fun of it. They be breaking out your windows. We saw a man—he was robbed, and he didn't have any clothes on."

The cops won't go inside: The white ones tell the outsider "you're crazy"; the black ones say "you're naive." Taking one of the elevators can mean an hour's wait; or worse, being trapped ten floors up with no way out. The stairs lead to muggings and rapes. At night, only the ear of the longtime resident can distinguish between the sounds of gunfire mingling with the slamming of hundreds of doors. It is a fearsome environment, out of human scale, a place of simple survival, constant noise, and random violence. For half of the children in Room 229, it is home.

"Someone is talking," Mrs. Thomas says pointedly. She puts her hand on her hip and looks across the classroom, a striking figure in her gray, high-collared pantsuit. "I should only hear the voice of the person to whom I have directed a question. Do not let me hear yours."

Black English is not spoken here; distractions are not tolerated; and reading is No. 1. Students have a set reading period every day, following a brief "warm-up" exercise. They get daily phonics drills and twice-a-day dictations, during which Mrs. Thomas reads and they write. In the tight half-circles of their reading groups, they have high-speed question-and-answer sessions. They take timed tests on skills such as spelling, looking up words in the dictionary, and subject-verb agreement. And they read aloud with inflection—all the periods, commas, question marks in their voices.

It's Friday, so there are a dozen new spelling words to be copied and kept in a folder: *dangle, telescope, anymore, spoke.* There are alliterations to be mastered: *pink pig, dirty dog.* "Oh people, let's get busy," Mrs. Thomas announces. "These papers will be completed today." There's work on figurative expressions: *running her mouth, being in hot water, hard-headed.* And there's a paragraph to be copied: *We're going to read about a funny little pig. His name is Greased Lightning . . .* "It's not so bad, so hard today," confides one of the third graders as he gets down to work. "Usually she doesn't have room on the blackboards for everything."

There are sentences to be parsed according to who, what, where, and when: *Beto lives in Mexico. Papa sat at the table.* And there are others which require a judgment as to whether they're facts or simply opinions: *There were thirteen colonies. I think she's pretty.* "Is it a fact just because I say it's so?" Mrs. Thomas asks her class. "Nooo," comes the cry in unison. "That's right," she fires back. "Of course, there're some things which are a fact if I say them—like, 'That work sure looks sloppy.' "

In one form or another, there is reading in Room 229 until at least 1:30 p.m. each day, leaving but an hour of school time for everything else. And always, the indomitable Mrs. Thomas is pushing, driving these very able, willing children over what she calls "the hump": reading at their grade level by midyear. "Oh people, let's hurry," she calls out. After all the *tests* are in April.

"Everything I do, I have a reason," she says. "Everything that's on the board relates to the skills that are on the tests. I don't particularly believe in the tests, but this is life and they have to take them and pass them in order to be promoted. I don't care how good a teacher you may think you are—if you're not zeroing in on what the child is to know, then you're not teaching.

"We don't sit around matching words; we read. If I can't get every child to read, I need help. I know what I'm expected to do, and I do it. I'm a teacher, and I'm expected to earn my salary and be responsible for certain things."

She strides to the classroom door, opens it, and motions out in the hallway. "You can't sit around your room here and do nothing. In Chicago, you can get away with that. But not in this school—this is a good school. Every teacher here is being held accountable; every teacher is doing it. They want to be here because this is where the kids are getting what they're supposed to be getting; the kids' parents want them to be here for the same reason. And guess what? This could be done anywhere—it doesn't matter what's across the street."

Recess begins, and Mrs. Thomas leads her children out to join the neat, no-nonsense lines of young students filing down Beasley's block-long main hallway. A group of eighth graders passes to their next classroom arranged by height, from the smallest to the tallest. "It looks nicer that way . . . and the kids like it," their teacher allows. A fifth grader spies two boys walking ahead of her, harmlessly scratching a capped pen along the concrete wall. *"They* should be *out* of *this* school," she offers, clearly embarrassed.

Around the corner, Arletta Cason's first graders march back to class from the bathroom. In the hour remaining before lunch, they'll have a dictation, a phonics drill, and some exercises on reading comprehension; after lunch, there'll be math, spelling, and a test on the day's skills. There won't be any "creative play," or arts and crafts, or cutting and pasting; and the children know it. First thing, they crowd around a large chart in the back of their room, checking and comparing their recorded progress in mastering reading skills. "They know what level they're on," Miss Cason says. "They know what they've accomplished. Every day the top group comes up and checks their place on the chart and every night the others go home saying, 'I'm going to be in that top group.' "

Beasley's janitor passes by on his way to turn off a fire alarm that's been tripped. He laughs to himself because he doesn't know which button to push. Except for drills, it's the first alarm to ring here in two years; at his last school, there were "15 or 20 false alarms a week, like clockwork." He isn't quite certain what to make of this place, with its walls free of spray paint, its huge papier-mâché bee sitting unmolested in the main corridor, its students and teachers lined up at the front door each morning to be let in an hour early. He likes it, except he's getting tired of having to get on the intercom every afternoon at four to ask everyone to leave for the day.

Down the hall, an eighth-grade discussion grows heated. "I'm going to prove my point," challenges the teacher, Virginia Dunbar. "You've got to prove yours." With that, one of Mrs. Dunbar's top students, Daphne Lave, is sent to the encyclopedia to settle the argument. Daphne smiles a bit wearily. "It's going to be a long day," she says. She did three hours of homework last night. She has three tests today—in social studies, science, and spelling. She's going to have to make a speech in one of her two English classes. But she says it's worth it: "It's kind of fun here really. You're expected to do more. I want to be the valedictorian of my class. It would be a good honor, a big honor. It's a challenge."

There's competition here—*academic* competition. Classes have "100s Clubs" for those with perfect test scores. Sixth-grade classes compete against each other for the highest spelling marks. Every student in the school memorizes a poem a week, and within some grades there are contests for the best presentations. "Nothing can stop this class," exhorts a poster hanging in an eighth-grade room. "I can do it," chants a first-grade class each morning after the Pledge of Allegiance. "I can do it, if I put my mind to it." An 11-year-old reflects on it all for a moment: "There's everything at this school." And his buddies chime in: "Yeah, you're supposed to act real smart; they make you real smart."

This is an oasis in a barren land.

This is the Beasley Elementary School—no, the Beasley *Academic Center,* Chicago's first "back-to-the-basics" school and the public school that has been hailed as a "lighthouse," a model for what urban education can be. This is the flagship of District 13, Chicago's poorest area. This is the school that works—the one with a waiting list, the top attendance rate, and some of the highest reading test scores in the nation's third-largest school system. This is the vivid product of Alice Blair's struggle to show that "these kids can learn."

* * *

Alice Blair, a plucky, 56-year-old grandmother, came home to head District 13 in 1976, bearing a hard-won reputation as a miracle worker and an educational philosophy best expressed by the sign on her conference room wall: "If God had wanted permissiveness, he would have given the Ten Suggestions."

She knew where she was going. She had been raised and had given birth to two of her three children in a home that was torn down when the slums were cleared to make way for the Taylor Homes. She had attended DuSable High, where her office is today. "We were very poor," she recalled. "We had the same kinds of problems as the kids in the area have now. It was a ghetto, but not a real ghetto like it is today. I didn't go to school with any white students; the schools were 100 percent black. But there was an economic mix; I was exposed to students from middle-class homes, to different standards. It led to my desire to go and make something of myself."

A church-sponsored scholarship enabled her to attend Knoxville College in Tennessee, but the money ran out after one year. World War II was on; she left college for the Women's Army Corps, in which she spent two years teaching conscripted dock workers how to read. The GI Bill provided the chance to go back to school to earn her degrees in education and embark on a career of some 20 years as a reading teacher, counselor, and assistant principal in the Chicago schools. In the early 1970s, she became the principal of the Manierre Elementary School, near the Cabrini-Green housing project just west of the city's center. Cabrini-Green ranks with the Taylor Homes; and Manierre was a mess. It's nickname was "manure." The kids were playing baseball in the halls; the school had had six principals in five years; test scores were more than just low, there were none. Mrs. Blair brought the place under control, earning herself some public acclaim and the superintendency of the 13,000-pupil District 13, one of 27 such divisions within the Chicago schools.

Mrs. Blair is short and heavyset. Her round face is framed by large glasses and a close-cropped Afro. Her voice has a soft, cultured tenor, but there is a firmness to it. She often is described as "tough" or "no-nonsense." Of Manierre, she said, "It was more hard work than a miracle." And faced with Chicago's lowest reading scores in District 13, her answer was much the same: "I just never knew there was such a problem getting kids to read. We just taught them. Now you hear it everywhere: 'These kids can't learn.' It's political. It's a self-fulfilling prophecy; I don't buy it.

"My biggest job here has been getting teachers and principals to believe all kids can learn. I didn't want them sitting around talking about the socio-economic situation of the children, what they had for breakfast and all that. I wanted them to know the skills they were to teach and to give the kids a lot of practice in those skills."

And so in the winter of 1977, Mrs. Blair laid down a series of mandates, not all of them written nor entirely in line with the rules of the Chicago schools. According to her decrees, every single class in District 13 would be reading at 9:30 every morning. The amount of time spent teaching reading each day would be doubled. Teachers would go over phonics charts stressing letter-sound associations and give dictations daily. Every school would use the same series of readers. Every principal would report monthly on each of his classes' progress. A cadre of reading consultants—Mrs. Blair's "storm troopers"—would float around the district, monitoring teachers' performance.

Every parent was sent a pamphlet, outlining Mrs. Blair's "Passport to Excellence Plus" plan. It called for a renewed emphasis on the three Rs, clear behavior and dress codes, regular homework, and a minimum reading achievement standard for promotion to high school (later adopted by Chicago at large). Parents were asked to sign individual "contracts" indicating their agreement and support.

Then came Beasley, her showcase and symbol.

No one wanted his kids to go to school at 52nd and South State streets, across from the Taylor Homes. Middle-class black parents didn't want their children to attend school with those from the Homes; they had protested at school board meetings to make sure they wouldn't be included when a new school was built in District 13. For Chicago's white parents, it was not a consideration, short of being bused there involuntarily (and the Chicago school board was dedicated to fighting the federal government on that score). Teachers—both black and white—were fearful, would not work there. A proposed school for the Beasley site had been on the drawing board for ten years with no action.

But Mrs. Blair was determined, and she "played all sorts of games to have that school built." She went downtown to meet with an all-white, all-male group of school administrators who candidly informed her "no one in this room would let their kids attend that school." She told them she intended to send her seven-year-old grandson there; "Oh well, you, you're different," they replied. She told them it would be a "back-to-the-basics" school, although the slogan as such didn't mean much more to her than a "marketing device." She called it a "kindergarten through sixth grade school with a middle-school component." She called it a "magnet school." She called it anything they wanted to hear. The name didn't matter. What counted was a greater-than-normal degree of control over who would work there.

Mrs. Blair ended up with an exceptional school building for kindergarten through eighth graders—one with orange-brown carpeting in some rooms, large windows overlooking a landscaped courtyard, science labs, separate band and choral music rooms, a swimming pool, a huge library. There had been new buildings before in Chicago, packed with plenty of frills. For Mrs. Blair, the building was gravy, a negligible factor compared to the power and simplicity of her concept: "My idea was that, if you could take a certain kind of principal committed to basic education, as many outstanding teachers as you could find and some parental involvement, then you could create an outstanding school—no matter where it was."

In her mind, the key was the school's principal. She had done her doctoral thesis on the professional qualities of principals of effective schools. And so she wanted someone who was a highly visible school leader, who visited classes often, who knew how to evaluate and work with teachers.

Beasley opened in the fall of 1978 with Bill McNerney—a plump, pixielike man with a quiet demeanor and a sharp eye for judging teaching talent—as that "certain kind of principal." McNerney, a principal in another District 13 school for 14 years, and Mrs. Blair are of vastly different temperaments; but they are of the same mind when it comes to how a school should be run.

Don't look for McNerney in his office; he spends his time wandering Beasley's halls, greeting students, watching and listening, particularly to that new teacher, that problem teacher. He hums to himself and smiles as he walks, and he invariably ends up where the action is. "He's where the teachers don't want him to be," said Mrs. Blair. "Every time I call over to Beasley, someone has to go find him, hunt him down. His monthly visitation reports are so detailed; other principals just check off—'I saw a social studies lesson.' With his, you can tell what the teacher was doing and not doing and what he's going to do about it."

Armed with the second important component of Mrs. Blair's formula for success—the special right to handpick two-thirds of his staff, twice the norm in Chicago—McNerney has set out to find and develop what he calls his "superstars," teachers like Maggie Brown Thomas. He goes and sits in the classrooms of other Chicago schools, observing and recruiting. "The first thing I look for," he said, "is a pleasant quality about the classroom—not 'open,' but not a stillness either. I want people who talk softly, who don't have to yell. And then there's kids raising their hands, papers posted of recent work, quickly graded work—all of which says to the children, 'I consider what you do important.' It's easy. Usually they're islands of sanity in their schools."

His eyes narrowed, his hands went up for emphasis. "Looking good as a principal depends mostly on your teachers. In Chicago, you've got some teachers who are prone to grievances or Monday viruses, or just kind of have a dead space between their eyes. Here, the teachers are good. I could drop dead today, and it wouldn't make much of a difference."

Lastly, Mrs. Blair rigged one other critical ingredient at Beasley, one that accounts for much of the school's success and at the same time clouds its virtues considerably: She put out a districtwide call for the best students.

District 13 principals didn't relish giving up what Mrs. Blair calls their "sparkplugs," their academic leaders. In some cases, they sent Beasley primary-grade children who didn't even know their names; about 70 children were sent back to their neighborhood schools. In the meantime, some black middle-class parents, many of them teachers, found out about Mrs. Blair's plans and pressured the school system to be let in. (Still many others called the school and when they were told its address, quickly hung up the phone.) Beasley began its first year, the 1978–79 school year, with about 1050 pupils: all black, about 80 percent from District 13, 65 percent from the Taylor Homes, and the lowest achieving not too far below their grade levels. One white child, a seven-year-old second grader and the son of a teacher at another south side school, showed up at midyear.

By the end of the year, Beasley's eighth graders had racked up the highest reading scores in Chicago, averaging more than a year above their grade level. Not one of them tested below the eighth-grade level and some were reading at the eleventh- and twelfth-grade levels. Beasley's first through seventh graders did not perform quite so well, but in every grade they averaged a year above the city's norm. The results did not go unnoticed. Droves of black middle-class parents now were interested; Chicago administrators named Beasley one of their "Access to Excellence" schools, a program geared toward encouraging voluntary desegregation.

Sudden success forced Mrs. Blair to tighten Beasley's entrance requirements. Children had to take special reading and math tests, submit samples of their work, and be accepted by a staff committee. In the 1979–80 school year, Beasley's enrollment from District 13 and the Taylor Homes dropped by about 10 to 15 percent, 28 white students took the bus there, and more than 900 black students from outside the district had to be put on a waiting list. The school's test scores again were among the top ten in Chicago, with every grade far above both local and national norms.

On the eve of Beasley's third year, it was becoming a private public school. As a "magnet" school, one drawing its enrollment citywide, Beasley was not unique, though. Magnet schools have been in some cities for many years. And they were a dominant educational trend in the 1970s, with such cities as Dallas, Milwaukee, and Cincinnati heavily investing in them as an attempt to provide voluntary desegregation and a reason for the middle-class to stay in urban school districts. By one estimate, some three million students attended such alternative schools in the 1978–79 school year. As a selective public school, Beasley also was not unique, although most other public schools with entrance requirements have been for high school students—Boston's Latin School and New York City's Bronx High School of Science, for example. Nevertheless, the problem with selective magnet schools—particularly when they draw much of their enrollment from a relatively small area, such as Chicago's District 13—is that they tend to skim off the best students from surrounding schools. And it is on this score that Beasley has come under fire.

"Beasley may be taking kids out of an environment of failure at other schools," said one Chicago school official who grows livid at the mention of Mrs. Blair and Beasley. "But it's creating nightmares in the schools from which it's draining the best students. It's a fraud, particularly if you're trying to make a statement about how to teach all kids. It's not an example of a successful school; it's an example of successful learners being lumped together. Blair is encouraging parents to believe if they can get their kid into Beasley, he'll become a genius. If they can get their kid into Beasley, the kid was learning all along. What I'm concerned about is the other 75 percent of the kids. What's happening to them?"

Indeed, the tragic side of Beasley may be that it was working in part because the last place that both its students and teachers wanted to return to was their neighborhood school—like the Terrell School two blocks away on State Street, where children ran wildly down paper-littered halls and spray paint decorated the outside walls. Terrell abuts the Taylor Homes; the school has the highest poverty ranking in Chicago. Reva Hairston, Terrell's principal, was diplomatic when asked about losing more than 50 of her top students to Beasley. She pointed out that Terrell prepared those students for Beasley, that other children have improved to replace them, that she has an eighth-grade class that's at its grade level. "We're not in competition with Beasley," she said. "We don't use it as a measuring stick. We don't say, 'If you do well, you'll be promoted to Beasley.'" But she also admitted that all of Mrs. Blair's mandates had not automatically improved the situation at Terrell: "It's the difference between what is, what should be, and what ought to be. We say, 'Hats off in the building and don't chew gum,' but, if the kids don't do it, we can't send them somewhere else like Beasley can. We have to deal with the problems."

District 13 test data showed that, following Mrs. Blair's arrival, its students' reading achievement average began to rise each year at about the citywide average rate of gain. But the district's average record included Beasley students from outside the area; and it was perhaps deceiving, for the achievement averages at Terrell and some other District 13 schools still were more than two years below national norms. As the Rev. William Vance, pastor of the Berean Baptist Church right across the street from the school, noted: "Beasley is in the community, but not of the community."

Chicago's interim school superintendent, Angeline Caruso, had doubts about Beasley, too. Mrs. Blair had the support of the previous superintendent, Joseph Hannon, who resigned in the fall, 1979, amid charges of financial mismanagement. But Miss Caruso has referred to Beasley as "exclusive for some, exclusionary for others." Under her direction, Chicago was not planning to create any more Beasleys. Instead, she was promoting an instructional quality control system called "continuous progress/mastery learning." The system, to be used at every school throughout the city, is geared toward all students, not just the academically able.

This plan, though, will be a long time taking hold throughout a half-million-student school system. And for most of Chicago's parents, particularly those in District 13, any criticisms of Beasley were purely theoretical; most other public schools simply couldn't compare.

For her part, Mrs. Blair remained unruffled, dismissing the criticisms as a "cop-out." She noted that District 13 was no longer last in the city's test scores, that 103 of the 110 pupils in Beasley's first eighth-grade class, which led the city in achievement, were poverty-level students from the district. She pointed to the achievement growth of students once at Beasley—sometimes two and three grade levels. And she said she'd like to start two more schools like Beasley. "When Beasley first started, it wasn't exclusive," she said. "We took kids from the Taylor Homes, the kids that no one wanted to go to school with. These children weren't learning anything in their other schools, they really weren't being challenged to work up to their capacities, to demonstrate how bright they could be.

"No one ever recognized that there were any bright students in this district before. Everyone automatically assumed that District 13 was the worst; well, we're not anymore. So the charge of elitism doesn't bother me. When a school in District 13 begins to be called 'elite,' I say that's something.

"In the lower-income areas of every city, there are literally thousands of kids with potential, locked into their housing projects and schools with no positive models. They're all looked at with the same eye, perceived to be the same; they're not encouraged; no one works with them. If nothing else, I've shown what these kids can do."

* * *

So Beasley may be an ideal world, but it's one with some real lessons. And the first concerns the social costs of writing off children. There are kids out there who want to work, who want what an effective school can offer—even amid what one teacher calls "the worst living situation imaginable."

There are kids out there like eighth grader Orlando Ruiz. Orlando, who reads as well as an eleventh grader, used to hate to go to school; his mother would have to kick him out of their ninth-floor Taylor Homes apartment each morning. Every afternoon she'd ask him what happened at school, and he'd just say, "Nothing." Now, he's so ready to go to school that when he got hit in the eye with a piece of glass, his mother had to force him to stay home for a few days. Now when he comes home after school, he goes right to the kitchen table and hits his books. "It's better at Beasley," he said. "They expect more, you do more. They trust you here. It's not that hard if you study, if you want to make it."

There are kids out there like Rick Rautanen, a white

eighth grader who came to a special summer school at Beasley between its first and second years and liked it so much that he stayed. Rick's family lives in what his mother called "a white stronghold" near the Indiana border, a neighborhood in which many Chicago police officers also reside. He said, "My friends say I must be crazy for going here. But I tell them if they could see what's going on here and were able to come, they'd want to go, too. They teach you here. At my other school, they just yelled at you. Here, they talk to you, treat you more like an adult, and you learn more."

At Beasley, Orlando's and Rick's teachers tell them what to do. They require hours of homework every night. They drill them, and they test them. Their teachers would call their homes if they were caught breaking any of the school's rules. If they were to be reported three times, they'd be put on probation. But Orlando, Rick, and Beasley's hundreds of other pupils don't seem to mind all that. And a 1980 Gallup survey commissioned by the Charles F. Kettering Foundation of Dayton, Ohio, suggests they are more reflective of their generation than might be thought: A majority of the teenagers surveyed—including two out of three black students—said the requirements of their public school were too easy. Just 19 percent of those surveyed said they were being asked to work too hard. And some 90 percent said they believe their teachers themselves should be tested regularly to see if they know what they're doing.

This last finding underscores Beasley's second lesson: That even within a heavily unionized, financially troubled, battle-weary system like Chicago's, superb teachers are still out there, too. There are hard-nosed, goal-oriented teachers like Arletta Cason, who "couldn't stand" her previous school, where "everyone was saying the children were dumb—don't bother teaching anything because they won't learn anyway." More than anything, these teachers want to be at schools like Beasley; some 400 were waiting for a spot on Beasley's 60-person staff. Said Jim Girton, the school's head teacher: "Teachers know they're going to be able to teach when they come here—not have to spend all day policing students."

But perhaps the overriding lesson of Beasley— particularly for those tempted to give up on the frustrating challenges facing the public schools—is that it is still possible to create a school in which teachers are personally accountable for how they spend their classroom time. Time is the most critical factor in learning, and most public schools simply squander it—with predictable results.

There are two ways to measure the use of the 1000 hours the typical student spends in his public school each year: by "allocated time," the time scheduled each day for each subject; and by "academic engaged time" or "time on task," the time students actually spend involved in learning these subjects. The two measures are not necessarily (nor usually) synonymous. The amount of school time allocated for academic instruction usually is set by state or local regulations, and so it is relatively constant within school districts; the percentage of that allocated time in which students actually are engaged in academic pursuits, however, varies widely from school to school. And it often is shockingly low.

For instance, a March 1979 survey by Austin, Texas, school administrators found that in their schools more than half of every instructional day of six and a half hours was devoted to noninstructional matters—discipline, recesses, bathroom trips, waiting for teachers' instructions, getting organized. Another study, by the Delaware Department of Public Instruction, found that teachers in some schools were spending up to one-third of the school day on "management tasks" alone. And a six-year-long study in California schools by National Institute of Education researchers during the 1970s found that the amount of "time on task" varied by as much as 100 percent among classes in the same grade level and that the total for reading and math combined was less than 100 hours a year in many classrooms. "Some students were getting something like 25 minutes a day in reading and 14 minutes in math," said Virginia Koehler, NIE's assistant director for teaching and instruction. "Some schools took six weeks to get their instructional programs off the ground." Added Tom Tomlinson, an NIE program officer: "Bad management has been teachers' historical prerogative."

But in study after study, it is the amount of this "time on task" that determines the degree of student achievement. In the August 1978 issue of the *Journal of Education,* a review of recent research on classroom instruction and student achievement by Barak Rosenshine, a widely respected University of Illinois professor, noted a clear pattern: Time spent directly on academic subjects and texts—as opposed to related games, puzzles, arts and crafts, stories or active play—correlates significantly with achievement. "Throughout these studies," he wrote, "there was no nonacademic activity that yielded positive correlations with reading and mathematics achievement. This result is somewhat surprising, because it has frequently been argued that some nonacademic activities contribute to academic gain by motivating students or by providing additional stimulation. Such indirect enhancement was not evident. . . . The message is, What is not taught in academic areas is not learned."

Rosenshine concluded: "Effective classroom teaching of basic skills takes place in an environment characterized by an emphasis on academic achievement. . . . Teachers who make a difference in students' achievement are those who put students in contact with curriculum materials and who find ways to keep them in contact."

This is an apt description of Beasley and its teachers. The

school's staff has one priority: the basic skills, reading in particular. And the school day has been restructured to provide more time—almost all day, if necessary—to achieve that goal. Pupils even can't take music, band, or art classes—"privilege classes," as they're called—unless they're performing satisfactorily in their academics. Any academic work they miss by taking one of these "privileges" they're required to make up as homework.

In class, Beasley's teachers don't mess around; they can't afford to. They're being watched, and they know it. Their conversations are peppered with "she ... she ... she"—constant references to Alice Blair breathing down their necks. For some, it's a fishbowl. "There's pressure on me and everyone here to perform," said Raelynne Toperof, who came in the school's second year. "It scared me a little at first." For others, however, it's innervating. "Teachers here always have to be doing something new," said Miss Cason. "If you don't, someone else will and you will be shown up." In either case, though, they know they are being held accountable for their students' performance. "She's difficult and demanding," Lillian Nash, Beasley's reading coordinator, said of Mrs. Blair. "But she's doing her job, and she expects you to do yours. You can't take a mental day off here; they don't leave you alone.

"We've had lots of money in the schools before, and machines to teach reading, reading through this and reading through that. But we've never had this kind of teacher contact with students. It's working, working because there's leadership."

Beasley has been working so well that the school's greatest problem will be limiting the hundreds of black middle-class parents, who despite their deep aversion to the Taylor Homes area, were clamoring to pull their children out of their neighborhood public and parochial schools and put them on a bus for 52nd and South State streets.

They've sent Mrs. Blair registered letters, beseeching her to let their children in. They've enlisted Chicago's aldermen to place calls on their behalf to Mrs. Blair and some board of education members. More than 1400 children were on a waiting list at the beginning of the 1980–81 school year.

But because school administrators made Beasley part of their voluntary desegregation plan, Mrs. Blair was under orders not to accept any more black pupils from outside District 13 until Beasley's enrollment becomes at least 10 percent white. For the overwhelmingly segregated Chicago schools, it was an ironic situation—black children being kept out of a black school that's in a black neighborhood. And it could become a sensitive issue, particularly if the numbers of children from District 13 also are limited in the future.

To avert this problem, Mrs. Blair has been working to draw enough white pupils. About 50 white students signed up for Beasley's third year, and Mrs. Blair was hoping that another dozen would be coming from the 11th Ward—a blue-collar area and former Mayor Richard Daley's homeground. "We're trying to keep it quiet," she said. "If there's publicity, their community would turn on them. With Chicago fighting busing, there's a great fear out there that if we show that voluntary desegregation can work, busing will be just around the corner. These people from the 11th Ward are not liberals; they just decided that Beasley offers what they want."

The parents' decision to opt for Beasley gives life to the most striking trend revealed during the first 11 years (1968 to 1979) that the Gallup organization polled public attitudes toward the nation's public schools: Each year integration and busing have been named as a major problem by significantly fewer people, while a significant increase has occurred in the number who cite poor curriculum and low standards as major problems. Among public school parents, almost twice as many cited low standards in 1979 as did busing. When asked what they liked least about their schools, their three most frequent responses were lack of discipline, low academic standards, and poor teachers. (The only difference between black and white parents surveyed was that blacks were even more critical of their schools than whites.)

The parents of Beasley's white students have found that it's the answer to these concerns, whatever the social risks involved in sending their children there. "We had to put up with a lot of static from the neighbors for sending him to school on the south side," said Maxine Rautanen, Rick's mother. "But the schools here are a big joke; the teachers, students, principal all think it's just so funny. Rick was screwing around, bored at his old school. They called him a behavior problem there; why is he acting so much better now? Beasley's unbelievable."

The school's black parents similarly have been impressed. "It has to do with structure," said Linda Colquitt, a teacher who pulled her third grader out of her neighborhood parochial school to take a 45-minute bus ride to Beasley. "He was doing his schoolwork in five or ten minutes. Then he'd look at the ceiling or play with his pencil. Now he brings home two-and-a-half hours of homework each night."

But Beasley has evoked the strongest allegiances across the street in the Taylor Homes. "All the parents say the same thing—Beasley's the best," said Orlando Ruiz's mother, Laura Duckworth. "I meet them in the grocery store, and they say Beasley kids are getting something extra, the teachers are giving more.

"I'm just thankful that Orlando was picked to go there. Everyone's trying to get their kids into Beasley."

Looking At Your School: The Basics

In attempting to apply this portrait of the Beasley Academic Center to other elementary schools, two themes are perhaps most prone to misreading: discipline and what's commonly referred to as "the basics." They're related, both in the classroom and in the public mind.

Discipline comes first; and well it should, for nothing else so much occupies the attention of educators and the imagination of the public as controlling the way kids act in school. Discipline tops the opinion polls every year as one of public education's biggest problems. In the 1979 Gallup survey, public school parents listed it twice as often as the next greatest perceived (and related) problem, that of drug use. And there are some real bases for this concern: Vandalism costs public and private schools more than $200 million a year and one of every 100 teachers in this country suffers an assault each month, according to a 1979 National Institute of Education report.

But the solutions advanced often reflect more of a martial mania than an educational effort, more of a concern with punishment than rewards, and more of an attempt to enforce obedience than promote self-control. And for these reasons, the efforts often produce results contrary to their intended aim of making school a better place to learn. "In many medium-sized and large cities especially, discipline has become a consuming issue and a siege mentality has developed about children and school," Susan Kaeser, an associate of the Cleveland-based Citizen's Council for Ohio Schools, wrote in a 1979 report, *Orderly Schools That Serve All Children.* "In some cases the public is hostile towards children and schools, and children are hostile about education and educators. . . . Many educators resign themselves to an unrewarding police role. Stricter discipline codes are written, more children are put out of school in efforts to create order, and educational dollars are spent on security guards."

School discipline programs that work rely on two simple principles: Kids, particularly those at the elementary school level, want to do well—no matter where they live or what experiences they have outside the classroom; and students who are kept busy, kept "on task," don't have time to get in trouble.

Well-behaving students, such as those at Beasley, are not the result of a system of discipline laden with rules and severe punishments. Rather, they are the product of an effort to make school a special environment, one with clear priorities. It is not simply that Beasley can ask misbehaving students to leave; it's that the school is a desirable environment for students to come to in the first place. Beasley makes explicit the behavior expected of students, and it rewards them accordingly. Responsibilities are stressed over rules. And those rules that exist are clearly stated and kept to a minimum, enabling consistent and reasonable enforcement. All of this is reinforced at home by a simple "contract," which each parent receives and signs.

Beasley teachers deal with behavior problems immediately as they occur in their classrooms. They do it without confrontation and without interrupting the continual flow of instruction. Research studies consistently show that effective teaching means fewer discipline problems. "Teachers who keep kids in touch with the curriculum, who move quickly from one subject to another, have more orderly classrooms," Virginia Koehler, of the National Institute of Education, said. "Theirs are not classrooms in the classic sense—with kids sitting with their hands folded neatly on their desks. They're ones in which everyone is working hard, the teacher's in control of the subject matter and is providing immediate reinforcement."

The message is clear and worth repeating: Discipline—

like student achievement—is a function of "time on task."
And so cutting down on wasted classroom time and improving the efficiency of instruction are the first steps toward
improving students' behavior. In attempting to promote better discipline among students, then, equal attention should
be paid to how well the adults in the schools are upholding
their professional responsibility to teach.

The public demand for stricter discipline often is accompanied by the cry of "back to the basics." And like attempts to
enforce better student behavior, educators' efforts to bring
their schools "back to the basics" often are more political
than instructional—and often just as misguided and ineffectual.

One of the biggest problems is that everyone knows what
"the basics" are—each in his own way. It is a term that has
been used so much and in so many different ways that it
quickly has become meaningless. Dennis Gray, associate
director of the Council for Basic Education in Washington,
D.C., the group that first introduced the term some 25 years
ago, likens its present-day popularity to the use of the "pro-life" banner by those opposing abortions: "No one can disagree with it; who isn't for 'back to basics'?" Gray views
the "educational conversation" as so polluted that the original concept of "the basics" is in danger of being confused
with myriad other concerns: the widespread call for orderliness and discipline; a drive towards stringency in funding
public education; the rise of the fundamentalist Christian
movement; a stress on the "3 Rs" to the exclusion of such
important subjects as science; an emphasis on vocational
or career-oriented education; and the two rising stars of
recent years, the "competency-based education" and the
"minimum-competency" movements.

But all of these have little to do with "the basics," as first
defined by the Council for Basic Education in 1956. At that
time, "life-adjustment education"—the notion that many

students were incapable of meeting academic challenges and so schools must attend to their social adjustment—was gaining popular support. ("Mathematics and mechanics, art and agriculture, history and homemaking are all peers," proclaimed a National Education Association report of the early 1950s.) The Council, now representing some 8000 members, viewed the "life-adjustment" movement as a kind of reverse elitism—"the handiwork of defeatists," in the words of one of its founders. And it advanced three propositions, which it still holds by: The primary business of schooling is academic, not social; "the aristocracy of basic subjects"—reading, writing, literature, mathematics, history, science, government, geography, foreign languages, and the arts—is inherently more worthwhile than other subjects, such as drivers' education and consumer education; and all children (except for the severely retarded) can learn.

"The basics," then, implies a concentration on a certain number of essential subjects—"those that have a generative power, that enable people to go on and learn whatever they want to learn later in life," according to Gray. If this has an old-fashioned ring to it or sounds elitist, remember that the Council argued—long before the Rev. Jesse Jackson cried, "Our children can learn, they must learn"—that even the most disadvantaged children can learn "the basics" and the schools should not settle for less.

And so the Beasley Academic Center is a "back-to-the-basics" school not so much because its students walk down its halls in straight lines or because they're quiet in their classes, but because the school reflects an unwavering commitment to academics, to high standards, and to the belief that no matter where children come from, they can learn. "The basics" at Beasley means setting priorities for schooling, making some hard choices about the most productive use of the school day, and making sure that instruction takes place. It means not writing off children.

2

All Kids Can Learn: *Mastery Learning*

At her desk in the rear of a second-floor classroom at the May School, Latrise Allen leans intently over her lesson on the 5 Ws: who, what, when, where, why. "Remember this when you're reading from a story or a paragraph," her teacher begins, following the mimeographed scripts in front of Latrise and each of the 25 other children in the class. "The title and the questions are the best clues to what the story is about. Sometimes they're not given. Then you have to make up your own questions. Some important ones to ask yourself are the 5 Ws."

Latrise and many of the other fourth, fifth, and sixth graders in the room move their lips and nod in agreement as they read along with Mrs. Hazel Claiborne. Then they quickly set to memorizing the next section of their scripts, a cartoon of a hand with each of the 5 Ws written at the tips of the fingers. "OK now, who wants to tell me what the 5 Ws are?" Mrs. Claiborne asks after about 20 seconds. Nearly every hand in the room shoots up, wiggling for attention, confident of the answer. "Who, when, where, why, and what," Latrise replies smartly.

"Is that right?" Mrs. Claiborne asks everyone. And together the children fire back, "Yes!"

That simple task accomplished, the day's lesson is off and running with every child in step. A sea of squirming hands meets every question; answers and immediate corrections fly back and forth. Together the whole class moves as a unit, flipping through the pages of its scripts. The children move through definitions of *who, when,* and *where,* and then through several paragraphs laden with these "clues":

> *Miss Jones called Jim's mother from school. Jim had started a fist fight with his friend Joe. His teacher was sure that Jim's mother would like to know about it.*

Through charts showing the relationships of characters (the *who*) in these stories:

NAME	WHAT YOU KNOW ABOUT THEIR RELATIONSHIPS
Miss Jones	*Jim's teacher*
Jim	*Miss Jones' student, a friend of Joe; had a fight with Joe*
Mother	*mother of Jim*
Joe	*friend of Jim; had a fight with Jim*

And through some exercises asking them to create "mental pictures" of actions (the *what*) described in other brief passages:

> *. . . make your mind behave like a movie camera. If you can "see" the story in your mind you will remember it more easily.*

> *EXAMPLE: Mrs. Kowalski's feet seemed to grow heavier with each step home. Her arms were full of groceries and she was so tired of carrying them. Suddenly Stan came whizzing around the corner on his skateboard, going too fast to stop. As he crashed into Mrs. Kowalski,*

*her groceries were flung all over the sidewalk. Even
though Stan apologized and helped her pick up the par-
cels, Mrs. Kowalski's face turned red with anger.*

*EXPLANATION: You should have made four separate
mental pictures: 1) Mrs. Kowalski walking with the
groceries, 2) Stan whizzing around the corner, 3) Stan
crashing into her with the groceries spilling and 4) Stan
apologizing to her as he picked up her groceries.*

Page after page, Mrs. Claiborne's students make their
way through similar, carefully calculated series of instructions, practice drills, and question-and-answer sessions, all
outlined in their scripts. In these small steps, they will
cover some 20 or more pages of the 5 Ws lesson over several
days until the students—almost every one—have mastered
inferring complex, unstated emotions (the *why*) from relatively lengthy reading passages:

*"You are so lucky, Annie," said Marlena as she
plopped down on the bed. "Your mom lets you stay out
late any night you want and watch as much TV as you
want. My mom makes me come home by 7:30—7:30!
Would you believe it? And I can't watch TV until I do
my homework," she moaned.*

*Annie had been staring out the window at the
shadows outside, thinking about what Marlena was saying. It was some time before she spoke. Finally she said,
"Yeah, I guess you're right in a way. But in another way
you are so much better off than I am. You can discuss
your problems with your mom and do things with her.
My mom lets me do anything I want because she doesn't
really care about me. All she cares about is playing
cards and talking on the phone. I hardly ever see her
much less discuss my problems." "Yeah," Marlena
agreed, "My mom really listens to me and sometimes
she's a big help."*

QUESTIONS:
> How would you describe Annie's feelings toward her
> mother?
>
> How would you describe Annie's mood?
>
> How would you describe Marlena's feelings toward
> her mother?
>
> How would you describe Marlena's mother?

Latrise Allen is sure that before the whole class moves on to its next lesson she will understand the 5 Ws just about as well as everyone else in the room. She knows that if she should fail to master this lesson the first time around, she will be given more practice time with another set of scripts that go over the same points in a different way, while her classmates read silently or review what they've learned. So she finds learning from these scripts "fun and easy. It's much better than just taking tests and not knowing what you're doing," she says, her eyes lighting up. "They've made me more confident. I know that I know the material. And when I get to the test, I'm not scared." For her teacher, Hazel Claiborne, the scripts solve a lot of problems. "They're so logical," she says after class. "Everything is here, step-by-step. They speak to kids at their level better; the kids end up more motivated."

These positive feelings should not be taken lightly, for what is happening here—in this all-black school on Chicago's rough west side—is something rather extraordinary for American public education, something of a revolution.

For one thing, this seemingly innocuous lesson on the 5 Ws deals directly with thinking skills that high-achieving students apparently acquire with ease, but that low achievers often fail to master. These skills, in either case, are rarely taught directly in the public schools. Second, Mrs. Claiborne is teaching to her entire class at once, and the pace of the lesson is being determined by the group as a whole. She is doing this irrespective of any individual differences in aptitude that may have been identified among her students. And she is doing this contrary to educators' traditional reverence for these differences.

Finally, all this is an experiment in which the Chicago public schools—a system of some 450,000 students—has entered into an unparalleled struggle: an attempt to equalize the opportunity to learn for every child in every one of its thousands of classrooms. It's called "mastery learning," and here it's at once a set of classroom lessons, a system of organizing instruction, and a philosophy based on a radical notion: *All* kids can and will learn.

Mastery learning, in its many variations across the country, holds the promise of classrooms in which achievement and its attendant rewards are not just the province of the top third, but of all students. Its proponents say it could reshape public education in ways that would have far-ranging social effects. In some cases, it is a sincere attempt to meet the needs of all students; in others, though, it amounts to just another hollow catchword. But whatever the case, mastery learning is threatening to become the fastest growing educational trend of the 1980s.

Mastery learning programs have been used in some small school districts—such as Johnson City, New York—since the early 1970s. Among large urban school systems, though, Chicago has developed and promoted the concept most extensively. By the start of the 1980–81 school year, some 4000 of the city's 17,000 teachers were trained in its principles; it was to be used in at least some classes in every one of the city's 500 elementary schools. And it was at the May School—an otherwise typical inner-city school with more than 1400 students in eight grades—that mastery learning gained a firm toehold in the Chicago public schools.

The May School sits by the Eisenhower Expressway near the city's western border. In the 1970s, its neighborhood went from predominantly white to more than 99 percent black; its crime rate soared to the highest in the city; and the climate at May deteriorated badly. By 1977, the school was in such a disorganized state that an assembly couldn't be held in its auditorium; its students, on the average, tested several years behind their grade levels; its staff members either were desperate or had simply given up.

But then Walter Thompson came to May as the school's reading coordinator, and he brought mastery learning along with him. Thompson had grown up in a Cincinnati ghetto, started school in one of that city's pre-1954 "voluntarily segregated" elementaries, and eventually made it to Harvard and his lifelong goal—teaching in urban public schools. Before coming to May, he had used mastery learning in a special Chicago summer school program for eighth graders who did not read well enough to be promoted to high school. He pirated the materials for use at May. "I saw its effects on kids," he says. "I knew it was needed. In the summer school, the kids were pushing me to learn, demanding even more work than I could give them. These kids were hungry, hungry to learn."

Thompson arrived at May the same time as the school's new principal, Albert Pranno, who had grown tired of "shuffling papers" as an administrator and wanted "to get back to something that provided some satisfaction." Thompson, a boundlessly energetic black man in his late forties, and Pranno, a stout Italian near retirement age, came together by chance, but they clicked. Pranno "never could understand why perfectly normal children didn't learn to read"; Thompson knew a way—finally—to teach them; and they joined forces to sell the rest of the May staff on mastery learning. "Walter and Al are a song-and-dance team," says one who worked closely with them. "They anchor the belief system at the school. Al provides the support, the resources, the love; Walter provides the order, the training. You should see them work a teachers' meeting."

Mastery learning was used in only a few classes at May in the 1978–79 school year. In most of these, students showed a year-and-a-half improvement in their reading test scores, while most of the school's other classes continued to gain a far more typical four to eight months. (One year, divided into ten "months," is the expected gain for each year in school on standardized achievement tests; students in Chicago and most other large urban school districts average about six to eight months gain each school year.)

In the 1979–80 school year, May became the first school in Chicago to have the program in almost every one of its classrooms. Of 31 mastery classes at the second-grade level or higher, about half showed gains of one year or better—with the top classes registering improvement of about two years. A quarter of the classes gained seven months or better (the citywide average). The remaining quarter improved less than seven months.

Pranno points to other measures of success, such as markedly better attendance and discipline. Also, about 50 May eighth graders gained admittance to Westinghouse and Lane, two of Chicago's elite vocational high schools (the first time any of the school's students had done so). "Children, parents, and teachers are starting to see progress," he says. "The child knows he's learning skills, moving from one level to another. He has pride; his teacher has pride; and, of course, his parents know it and have pride." Even with all that, Pranno won't call mastery learning a panacea for the problems of urban schools: "You've got to believe in it, be able to use it correctly. There's got to be support. Without that, you'd just be going through an awful lot of silly motions. It would be another program spinning its wheels."

But Thompson takes a look around May—where students' median family income is about $6900 a year, where almost

40 percent of the pupils transfer in or out of the school each year—and predicts in no uncertain terms: "We're going to look like a suburban school in a few years, performance and testwise. This is built on success. It teaches the child to think. It takes good teachers and makes them great, and it makes competent teachers of poor ones. Up to now, what we've had in the classrooms are kids and teachers who know they're not going to succeed. Up to now, all we've been doing is just failing kids."

* * *

Chicago's path-breaking commitment to mastery learning began in 1975 as an attempt to apply a new body of research on students and learning to the harsh realities of urban classrooms. It was founded on a simple, but distinctly different model of school learning first developed in 1963 by educational psychologist John Carroll. Instead of smart and stupid students, Carroll theorized, there are only faster and slower learners. Aptitude tests, he said, measure only the time a student would require to master a subject to a given level; they do not predict intelligence, or an absolute limit on what a student can learn. With enough time, Carroll believed, every student could master subjects to a set level.

He noted that providing the same amount of learning time to all students is tantamount to guaranteeing that achievement will fall in line with the familiar bell-shaped curve yielded by aptitude tests. However, if the amount of learning time were adjusted for each student according to his need, then Carroll said the pattern of achievement would be skewed to the high end of the scale, and there would be no relationship between achievement and aptitude.

Consider how sharply Carroll's ideas contrast with the model of learning that prevails in most school systems: Intelligence is a permanent characteristic of each individual; it's a capacity that some students have more than others; so the wide range of achievement displayed in school merely mirrors the normal range of intelligence, and there's little anyone can do about it. Readiness tests, achievement and ability groupings, grading and selection systems, curriculum, course organization, guidance counseling procedures all spring from this concept. Most compensatory education programs are based on it, and so are most teacher training programs. Indeed, public schools can be viewed as great sorting machines dedicated to weeding out poor learners from their better peers, who then are encouraged to learn as much as possible.

However, in the 1960s, Benjamin Bloom, a University of Chicago education professor, began to develop an instructional model based on Carroll's concepts, a model in which individual differences in school achievement are viewed as man-made, often accidental, and definitely not fixed in time. In his book, *Human Characteristics and School Learning*, Bloom took Carroll's model to its radical conclusion: Ninety-five percent of all students can master what only the top students had been expected to learn. It was an optimistic vision of nearly error-free schools, one that discounted the idea of good/poor learners as well as Carroll's concept of fast/slow learners. "Most students become very similar with regard to learning ability, rate of learning, and motivation for further learning," he wrote, "when provided with favorable learning conditions." And in his experiments, he developed a way to provide these "favorable conditions," the heart of the mastery learning strategy:

1. Specify concrete objectives for what is to be learned and divide these into small, sequenced units.

2. Provide instruction and student practice for one unit at a time, and then administer a test—not for grading purposes, but to check on which objectives students have mastered and which require more study time.

3. Based on each student's errors on the test, provide

individual "prescriptions"—a second chance to learn the objectives through a different means of instruction. (Students who have mastered the objectives spend this time studying on their own.)

4. Last, administer a second test to check on the progress of those students who had been given a second chance to learn.

Bloom's model differs from traditional instruction in four critical ways. Learning time is altered to fit the task, rather than squeezing the task into a preset time. The second chance to learn is offered as a way of providing "private tutoring" within the typical class of 30 or more students. Tests are no longer situations in which students compete against each other for limited space at the high end of the normal grading curve; tests now are part of the learning process. Teachers no longer serve as passive classifiers of students; they now are students' active partners in learning—they must specifically address student failure.

Bloom found this instructional strategy led most students to master at least 80 percent of the objectives of every lesson. And just as importantly, students then went on to the next lesson with a greater command of prerequisite skills and a higher level of motivation. In essence, he found that mastery learning produces a J-shaped curve of achievement, one in which very few students end up at the low end of the achievement scale and one very different from that produced by most schools.

The cost of these benefits is that more time is required to teach this way than when traditional methods are used. Bloom found the slowest students initially need as much as five times more learning time as the fastest students in order to master 80 percent of the objectives; as they proceed through the lessons, though, this drops rather quickly to a two- or three-to-one ratio. Among college students, with whom most of his early experiments were conducted, this was not a great problem, for they were able to study on their own and find the extra time within their schedules. But it was a seemingly defeating requirement for those at lower grade levels, where learning time is subject to many more constraints.

Although Bloom's theories were the subject of much research and interest, they remained just that in the United States until one of his former graduate students, Michael Katims, took on the massive challenge of translating mastery learning into a day-to-day reality for the Chicago schools. Whereas Bloom had been the careful scholar, Katims, an intense 33-year-old, was to play the impatient engineer.

Katims first attempted to devise a mastery learning program around the commercially published series of basal readers used in every school. This method failed, however. Most readers are hopelessly weak when it comes to a clear focus on skills, a sequence of skills, and related practice. Teachers had trouble sequencing the material on their own; far too many pupils failed the initial tests; and correcting students' mistakes became an unwieldy, overly time-consuming matter.

So Katims and his associates—from a diverse range of backgrounds, including a former secretary, a junior high teacher, a professional writer, and the author of an Israeli text on English—began writing their own instructional materials, hundreds of pages of scripts like those used at the May School. It was new ground, something that even Bloom had not envisioned. Their goal was to create a "teaching machine without the machine," one that could be used inexpensively with all students in every classroom, with good and bad teachers, and within the confines of the regular school day. Additionally, their work had to fit into Chicago's newly adopted system of "continuous progress," an outline of 1400 separate instructional objectives in four different areas of reading (word attack, study skills, comprehension, and literature).

Of these 1400 criteria, 273 were designated as essential; and criterion-referenced tests were developed to evaluate students' mastery of them. By 1978, Chicago's eighth graders were expected to master 80 percent of these key objectives in order to gain promotion to high school. Despite the promotion requirement, continuous progress did not get off to a fast start in the system's classrooms. Skill charts were distributed to teachers, along with administrative goals as to students' expected progress. Many teachers ignored both the charts and the goals; for others they were just another source of frustration. As one teacher put it: "It was a terrible feeling to be in class and not have your students master the skills fast enough. There was nothing you could do." Nevertheless, Katims viewed mastery learning as a tool to make continuous progress work: "Continuous progress is the 'what,' what students are supposed to learn; the criterion-referenced tests tell you 'when,' when they've learned it; and mastery learning is the 'how,' how you get them there."

The mastery learning materials Katims created to fit the continuous progress system adhere to Bloom's principles. Each lesson comes with two or three teacher-led activities (the scripts), student practice sheets, diagnostic tests, reteaching exercises for those failing to master the objectives the first time around, and additional activities for those achieving mastery right away. The learning goals for each lesson are explicit. There are provisions for immediate correction of students' errors by the teacher; the reteaching exercises use a different approach in presenting the material a second time.

Also, materials for the upper grades (five through eight) attempt to lead students through the thinking steps used in solving more involved problems, such as making comparisons and understanding symbols and analogies. Students are provided with clear-cut strategies for comprehending material, as in the portion of the 5 Ws lesson that urged Latrise Allen and her May School classmates to make "mental pictures" of the actions described in stories. These lessons, developed by Katims' associate Beau Jones, are based on the research finding that the fundamental difference between high-achieving and low-achieving students is that the top pupils spontaneously develop certain thinking skills and learning tactics while their less successful peers do not. This divergence in thinking styles normally occurs between the fourth and sixth grades according to the research, about when reading test scores in most urban school districts fall off precipitously.

Previous research experiments with mastery learning—the most extensive were conducted in South Korea with thousands of students in classes of 70 or more—have shown that mastery pupils consistently outperform those receiving traditional instruction. In two major tests in Chicago, the results have been similar. The first was the summer 1978 program in which Walter Thompson taught. In that summer school, 10,000 eighth graders—all of whom were behind in their work—gained almost as much in their test scores after seven weeks of mastery learning lessons as they had during the previous nine-month school year with traditional instruction. But Katims did not want to talk about "numbers of students and classes. I wanted to show mastery learning worked with an entire school," he said, "that it could create a school that works." So the May School was the second test, and Katims got the results he sought, virtually assuring Chicago's commitment to the program. Despite the school system's grave financial problems, he was predicting in 1980 that within three or four years Chicago's classrooms would be saturated with mastery learning materials.

"We're going to build super schools everywhere in this city," he said. "It's not going to happen next year or in two years, but 10 or 20 years down the road. For the first time, we'll really be able to take a look at what individual differences mean. 'Til now, individual differences in school have just been a mask, an expression of family background, socio-economic status or race. Now we can begin to really work on opening up real options for children.

"As soon as everyone can be taught to read at a certain level, they can do what they choose—not what society has prepared for them."

* * *

This issue of equality perhaps disturbs educators the most. "The utopian vision of mastery learning is not really a radical change in schooling, but instead it's what teachers concerned with subject matter have always wanted—30 students of equal ability who need one lesson plan for all," Carl D. Glickman, a University of Georgia professor of education, wrote in the November 1979 issue of *Educational Leadership* magazine. "Even if it 'works' we still need to ask ourselves if we want students to be equally masterful of the same skills and knowledge. This is an important question because what is or what can be is not necessarily what should be."

Many educators tend to be taken with "humanistic" philosophies and, by the same token, attach stigmas to models of learning that teach all children the same way, models that smack of "behaviorism." The research of Jean Piaget, Jerome Bruner, and others—stressing the different stages of children's cognitive development—retains much influence. Educators often worry about the singular child with unusual talents as much if not more than the great mass of children struggling to learn how to read. Chicago's continuous progress/mastery learning program, thus, has been criticized as too mechanical, oppressively dull and intellectually stifling.

There are also many who doubt whether teaching atomized, easily digested reading skills amounts to teaching kids to read. Even Alice Blair, who couldn't agree more with Benjamin Bloom that all kids can read if taught properly, calls continuous progress "a flop. If you just teach these discrete bits of skills," she said, "classes won't learn anything." And there are further, practical difficulties with mastery learning, among them the problems of reaching agreement on educational objectives, designing effective tests to measure mastery, and developing efficient remedial strategies. Teachers in Chicago also have resisted the increased record keeping that goes with the system. Because they perceive themselves to be working at full speed already, they find it hard to imagine where they can carve out the additional 10 to 20 percent more teaching time required by the program. The greatest fear stimulated by mastery learning, though, is that, since it promises all kids can learn, it could lead to a strict system of teacher accountability for student achievement.

Even Walter Thompson, who is sold on the program, advises that mastery learning should not be introduced too quickly or all at once to a school. Teachers resist change, he says, primarily because they are hooked on basal readers even when it's evident that they don't work. He suggests not discarding the basal readers entirely and using a careful approach in introducing mastery learning, one that starts with a few carefully selected teachers. Nevertheless, at May, mastery learning gained quick acceptance once it began to produce results. Teachers began to ask for each of the lessons as they were written; they copied them from each other. And Thompson and Katims say it's because the lessons directly address the most serious problems of urban classrooms:

Belief

"Success begats success" is mastery learning's motto in Chicago. "If you can demonstrate to teachers that kids can learn," Katims said, "it can have a shattering effect on them." The same holds true for students. It commonly is assumed that motivation on the part of students leads to achievement, but Barak Rosenshine's 1978 review of the research on classroom instruction and student achievement concluded that motivation is the product, rather than the source, of achievement. To this end, each mastery learning lesson builds in success by beginning at an achievable, familiar level and proceeding in small steps to the increasingly complex and unfamiliar. For example, a fourth-grade lesson on topic sentences starts with classifying groups of objects (*Can you think of one word that describes apple, pear, grapefruit and plum?*), moves to a definition (*. . . the sentence that tells you what the other sentences are about*), and ends with students identifying topic sentences buried in long paragraphs.

"Good students make good teachers more than the other way around," Katims said. "We now send teachers into classrooms, where the kids are three to four years behind, armed with a piece of chalk and some readers. The students don't believe in themselves; the teachers are fearful of being held accountable for their progress. The way out is to create opportunities for success. When kids fail in mastery learning, they don't get kicked down. They don't get further behind. They get reprogrammed for more learning."

Expectations

A firm classroom axiom is that students do what is expected of them. Students typically do not face a clean slate with each new school year; as a rule, teachers already have formed opinions about their classes and particular students that serve to determine who is worth teaching and who is not, with commensurate results. Perhaps the most powerful study illustrating this pattern was *Pygmalion In the Classroom*, published in 1968 by Robert Rosenthal and Lenore Jacobson. The researchers told teachers at a San Francisco elementary school that about 20 percent of their students had been singled out by a test as having an unusual potential for "spurting," or rapid intellectual growth. Eight months later these same students, who actually had been randomly selected, showed significantly higher I.Q. gains in contrast to their peers in the same classes. The researchers concluded their work by quoting from G. B. Shaw's play, *Pygmalion:* ". . . You see, really and truly, apart from the things anyone can pick up (the dressing and the proper way of speaking and so on), the difference between the lady and the flower girl is not how she behaves, but how she is treated."

Thompson agrees. "More and more, I've come to realize that what we have in inner-city schools is differentiated service," he said. "So very many times, educators assume children can't learn because of their environment or whatever. They're all too ready to accept the fact a child can go only so far. When I came to this school, some teachers told me that two-thirds of their students were handicapped mentally. I asked them how they knew that; they said they just could tell."

But mastery learning reverses the traditional system of instruction, so that the pupils who need more instruction get it. And Thompson believes it forces teachers to stop making damaging distinctions among children—whether on the basis of race, social class, appearance, I.Q. tests, or previous achievement records. "Getting to some adult attitudes is a trip," he said. "But I've seen racist teachers— one in particular, we used to call 'the plantation owner'— turn themselves around with mastery learning. The kids do it; they push the teachers to teach."

Quality Instruction

A wide variety of observers across the country believe that the single greatest problem afflicting the public schools is the quality of its teachers and their work. When asked, "In your opinion, what are the main things a school has to do before it can earn an A?," respondents to the 1980 Gallup Poll of public attitudes toward the public schools listed first "improve the quality of teachers." Graham Down, executive director of the Council for Basic Education, said flatly: "The single greatest problem with the schools is the illiteracy of teachers—40 percent of them can't do their jobs." Thompson believes it, too: "A large number of teachers shouldn't be teaching kids. Teacher training institutions are producing people with credentials. For what? Not for teaching. It's an art; You have to know how to instruct with kids in mind. I try to tell a lot of teachers they should be selling shoes."

What should teachers be doing differently? To repeat Barak Rosenshine's conclusion: "What is not taught in academic areas is not learned." Effective teaching, he said, is characterized by a high amount of "time on task," a strong academic focus, and a pattern of direct, explicit instruction. "Direct instruction" is defined as presenting lessons in small steps at the students' level, providing a great amount of work that is mediated directly by the teacher, and offering many opportunities for students to venture answers and to find out if they're right or wrong. As the National Institute of Education's study in California's schools concluded: "The critical problem is not whether a teacher teaches in a group; it is whether such teaching provides direct instruction to pupils."

One of the main reasons for the widespread failure of elementary school teachers to provide this quality of instruction is their heavy reliance on basal reading series. Basals often are widely promoted without much concern for their effectiveness; they often do not teach what they purport to teach. For instance, five of the best-selling series give little attention to instruction in reading comprehension, according to unpublished research by Dolores Durkin, of the University of Illinois. Their teaching "manuals give far more attention to assessment questions and written practice than to direct, explicit instruction," she found. Not surprisingly, this conclusion is in line with an earlier classroom-observation study by Durkin in which she discovered that elementary school reading and social studies teachers provide "almost no comprehension instruction [and] . . . instruction other than that for comprehension was also rare." Instead of teaching students, she found, teachers were spending their time giving, explaining, and checking assignments.

Mastery learning, as it has been developed in Chicago, weans teachers away from their familiar reading books through the use of scripts that involve consistent patterns of instruction, drill, feedback, and questions. It literally mandates more efficient use of classroom time, a high degree of "time on task" for students, and direct instruction. "It demands that teachers instruct kids in a certain way," said Thompson. "They have to participate in their learning. It's pretty hard for them to mess it up."

*   *   *

The teachers were skeptical. After all, they teach in New York City's high schools. And here was this woman—the superintendent of a New Jersey school district with just 1000 students—telling them the whole idea of reading levels is a "false concept" for high school students, that the tenth grader who tests on the third-grade level actually knows a lot more than that. "With mastery learning," she was telling them, "you just worry about the objectives and what you have to do to teach them. If it's that important for the kids to know the material, then you have to pull them up to that level."

She practically was hooted out the door of the eighth-floor classroom at Manhattan's Norman Thomas High School. "When in the hell are you supposed to find the time to get all this done?" asked a social studies teacher. "I know the kids I face. Out of 35, maybe five read at grade level. I've got maybe ten different grade levels in each class; what am I supposed to do—write out ten different ways of correcting students' mistakes? I only get paid to teach five hours a day."

Another teacher added: "It's all great, but how can you do this when you don't have enough books for every kid?" And one muttered to himself: "I hear they got a new program, Students for Higher Intellectual Training—S.H.I.T."

But after Joan Abrams, the superintendent of the Red Bank, New Jersey, schools left the room, the 20 social studies teachers immediately went to work, ripping apart and reorganizing their textbooks into small chunks of material according to Benjamin Bloom's principles of mastery learning. They have seen a lot of new programs come and go, and always it's the teachers that get blamed—"the poor guy on the front line, busting his chops," as one put it. But remarkably, they are not without hope. "I'd really like to see mastery learning work," said one of the teachers who had just been complaining most vociferously. "If I can improve my classes just 5 percent, then it would be worth it. . . ."

On this summer day there was the same mix of belief and doubt, enthusiasm and wariness running through the high school's other classrooms where 80 more New York City teachers were in the middle of a four-week training session on mastery learning. They had not been told that mastery learning, in essence, throws the responsibility for student achievement back on teachers. They had not been told anything about changing their styles of teaching. Instead, they had been taught how to ferret out the objectives of their lessons, how to write criterion-referenced tests to measure whether students have mastered these objectives, and how to develop "correctives," materials to address student failure. Each of them was doing for himself what Michael Katims and his associates have done for Chicago teachers: writing mastery learning curricula.

"We don't hit them over the head with lots of principles and theory," said Thomas Guskey, who had been brought in from the University of Kentucky to lead the training program. "We work on changing their behaviors, rather than their attitudes. No teacher will leave this workshop truly believing that all kids can learn. But many of them—particularly the ones who are most cynical now—will come back as true believers."

Guskey studied under Bloom and served two years in the research and evaluation office of the Chicago schools, where he became familiar with the continuous progress/ mastery learning system. But he favors a different and perhaps more palatable form of mastery learning: programs developed directly by the teachers who use them, rather than by a small group of specialists. Mastery learning programs developed by teachers themselves naturally are slower to introduce on a large scale; there also are real questions as to whether teachers—whose quality of work is suspect in the first place—can become proficient at writing instructional programs. Michael Katims says this method suffers from requiring teachers to "make too many decisions for which they're not prepared." Guskey, though, believes what this method sacrifices in speed and consistent quality is more than compensated by the high level of teacher commitment and the lasting changes it promotes.

Powers within New York City's United Federation of Teachers, the school system itself, and the Economic Development Council of New York, an organization representing some of the city's largest corporations, have accepted Guskey's line of thought. In an unprecedented partnership, the three groups have set out to permeate five key high schools—one in each borough of the city—with mastery learning materials developed by these schools' own teachers. Their jointly sponsored summer training programs started small with eight teachers in 1978 and grew to include 28 more teachers in 1979 and another 100 at Norman Thomas High in 1980. Organizers were predicting about 25 ninth- and tenth-grade teachers will have been trained at each of the five high schools by the end of the 1980–81 school year and mastery learning curricula will have been completed for six subjects—English, biology, algebra, geometry, Spanish, and Italian.

The support of the teachers' union—the most powerful force in the New York City schools—cannot be underestimated in all this. But the business-funded, nonprofit Council has played a unique role. Previous to the training programs, the Council had placed full-time consultants in 29 high schools and launched a search for "proficiency-based" instructional programs that work, such as mastery learning. "Mastery learning makes sense to corporations because it stresses student outcomes—that's how business trains people," said Lloyd Cooke, the Council's vice-chairman on loan from Union Carbide, where he was director of community affairs.

Cooke used to be a research chemist; he works with the U.S. Office of Technological Assessment, a congressionally mandated group that studies the effects of new technologies as they seep down through society. So he has some experience in studying the best way to introduce new methods: "One of the main reasons that 'turn-key' plants [totally new facilities built from scratch] often fail is because there's a cultural gap between the technology and the workers. The process is like a skin graft—either the technology is accepted or repelled.

"With mastery learning, you can't start by telling the teacher that he's going to have to change; you stay away from any suggestion that it's a different way of doing things. Most teachers don't believe that all children can learn. They are tyrannized by the normal curve of distribution; there's nothing in their background or much on record to enable them to consider kids in any other way. It frightens them. So you do it in steps. First, you just tell them they're going to add a few things to what they normally do within their existing context. Then, you have to give them time to get some results. Once they see that their students actually can learn, then they begin to believe it."

Cooke points to JHS 227, Shallow Junior High in Brooklyn, as an example. Shallow is in an Italian, blue-collar neighborhood; about 75 percent of its students are white. Mastery learning began there in the 1978–79 school year after three of the school's teachers were trained in the first summer program; within two years, the testimony of those using mastery learning had been so favorable that 22 of Shallow's teachers signed up for training. "My classes are doing 20 percent better now; the distrust factor between my students and me has disappeared," said Lou Leonini, a 35-year-old social studies teacher, who was among the first three teachers trained. That first year, Leonini had one mastery class and another "control group" receiving traditional instruction. Halfway through the year he had a crisis of conscience: "Mastery learning was working so well I had trouble denying it to the control group, and I ended the experiment." At the end of the year, his seventh graders petitioned Shallow's principal to continue with mastery learning in the eighth grade. Said the principal, Donald DelSeni: "Mastery learning sells itself."

Its success at Shallow, along with the financial and political support of the teachers and business organizations, seems to have assured mastery learning's growth within the New York City schools, just as it has won support in Chicago. And the rising public demand for urban educators to set and have their students meet competency standards may well propel mastery learning to the forefront in public schools all across the country in the 1980s. At least a dozen school districts, including New Orleans and Denver, reported using mastery learning programs by 1980. Educators, however, have a way of adopting a trendy slogan without really making fundamental changes in the classroom. Already "mastery learning" is becoming a catchword, one often confused with "competency-based" and "individualized" education. Although the concept is clear, the practice of mastery learning often is colored by local conditions. It is still up for definition. And so a diversity of philosophies, approaches, and effects have been subsumed by its banner, as shown by these profiles of four relatively small systems that adopted programs in the 1970s.

District 19, Brooklyn

"It's too early to tell if it's going to work, but it's better to light candles than curse the darkness," Leon Weisman, director of reading for District 19, said in the middle of the 1978–79 school year, mastery learning's first there. By the next summer, however, Weisman was seeing some remarkable changes: "A reading fervor has overtaken this district; teachers now sit in the lunchroom talking about how to teach reading; it's become the prime concern." He already credits mastery learning with reversing the steady decline in the district's reading test scores: About 29 percent of its 25,000 (predominantly black and Hispanic) pupils were at or above their grade levels in reading in 1979; that figure jumped to about 36 percent in 1980. Instead of training teachers to write their own programs, District 19 bought the materials developed by Michael Katims in Chicago, and Chicago consultants were brought in for one-day sessions in which 160 third- and fourth-grade teachers and 30 eighth-grade teachers were trained. Weisman planned to train every one of the district's 1500 teachers and turn all its first-through eighth-grade classes over to mastery learning. Reading time in the district's schools already had been doubled; and in mastery classes, teachers were using basal readers only about 40 percent of that time. The changes were made quickly. "It takes a long time to become a good program writer," said Weisman. "The choice was between becoming a gourmet cook or buying your food frozen. What choice did I really have? We decided to buy frozen."

Red Bank, New Jersey

Ruth Abrams, a former elementary school principal in New York City and superintendent of this small school district for six years, took an approach opposite to District 19's, mandating that her teachers write their own mastery learning materials. She heard Benjamin Bloom speak in 1977 and immediately lined up her school board behind his concepts. "The community liked the idea right away," she said. "But the teachers' union took out ads saying we were going to restrict their academic freedom and teachers started dragging their feet. I said, Look at our [low] test scores—you call this academic freedom?" Finally, the school board sent letters to the district's 100 teachers, telling them they would be required to use mastery learning materials in the 1979–80 school year. As a result, Red Bank's fifth- through eighth-grade reading test score averages improved from one-half year to a year and a half. "The biggest surprise," Abrams said, "was the unwillingness of teachers to be accountable. They wanted to do less, rather than more. They believed that students couldn't learn."

Red Bank is an urban center of 18,000 residents on the

New Jersey coast, halfway between New York City and Atlantic City; Abrams says its pupils range from "the barely surviving to the very top, with all the problems in between." Nevertheless, the district has adopted the classic mastery learning model: All classes are composed of students at a variety of ability levels; instruction is directed at the whole group; and classes do not progress until almost every student has mastered the lessons. "We used to give reading tests, get grade levels, and then gear all instruction to those [low] levels," Abrams said. "Now, we instruct at their [normal] grade levels. We've found that some kids never received much instruction before; it was the teachers that were holding them back."

Johnson City, New York

A white, blue-collar school district of 3000 students in upstate New York, Johnson City has had experience with mastery learning at both the elementary and secondary levels since 1971. In that time, its students' test-score averages in grades one through eight have shot up as much as a year above national norms; on New York's competency tests (in grades three and six), Johnson City pupils have improved 10 to 15 percentile points and rank well above both the county and statewide averages. Both methods of mastery learning are used there: teacher-developed materials in high schools and prepared materials at the elementary level. In either case, Superintendent John Champlin, who brought mastery learning there, stresses, "What's important is a philosophical commitment, an attitude about the material and kids. It takes a long time to develop, but it begins to attack some of the basic premises of school; you don't just bring kids in and fit them to a preconceived curve." Along these lines, he's also found that mastery learning is "no poor man's technique. We don't separate our gifted kids," he said. "We've built mastery programs for everyone that include high-level activities for these [gifted] kids. Their presence in the classroom invigorates the entire class; they add strength and quality."

Lorain, Ohio

This 14,000 student (40 percent Hispanic and black) school district about 25 miles west of Cleveland has had full-scale mastery learning programs in math at the elementary level since 1977 and at the secondary level since 1979. But Nicholas Hutlock, director of these programs, began developing them in 1971. "Mastery learning doesn't do away with all your problems—new ones just come up," he said. For instance, when he started, he discovered that 15 different teachers at the district's five junior highs were using 15 different math programs. In the district's English classes, where development of a mastery learning program has been stalled because no one can agree upon a set of critical skills, no less than 75 programs are in use. Mastery learning also has forced changes in what Hutlock calls the district's long-standing "hush, hush system of tracking kids. You know, we'd test them in junior high and put some kids in certain courses and they'd go to college; and then we'd put the rest in other courses and they'd get to work at Ford." And mastery learning had prompted a look at the way time, credits, and courses are organized in Lorain. "Schools can't figure out what to do with kids who finish a course in midyear or the ones who need extra time to master their work," Hutlock said. But even with the problems, he believes "there's no question that mastery learning works. The issue is how do you change the basic assumptions of school systems—their organizational structure—to provide instruction? Schools aren't set up for kids to learn."

To address some of these issues, eight school districts involved with mastery learning or similar programs—including Johnson City, Red Bank, and Chicago—banded together in 1980 to form a national Network for Outcome-Based School (NO-BS, for short). "We set up the group because—with the magnitude of mismanagement in this business—we were concerned that mastery learning would go down the drain, the hucksters would move in and nothing would be changed," said John Champlin of Johnson City. The group has drawn up a list of some common philosophical principles and "operational essentials," including: Almost all students are capable of achieving excellence; effective instruction varies the time needed for learning; it's necessary to state goals publicly and key them to an objectives-based curriculum. But these statements are so broad as to include programs not exactly in line with the original concept of mastery learning.

For example, the New Orleans schools, a member of the Network, has 30,000 seventh through twelfth graders in a "mastery learning" program that essentially amounts to a continuum of objectives along which each student moves individually. It does not involve whole group instruction nor an effort to reduce the wide spread in achievement produced in school. It is more of a management system, a way of keeping track of children's progress, than anything else. "The teacher is more of an organizer and manager than an instructor," said Carmen Dolese, New Orleans' director of secondary education. "You can't really do group-based instruction in an urban setting; you'd have to worry about holding some kids back."

The Network's vision of mastery learning is so all-encompassing that it also embraces competency-based education. "Mastery learning is the kind of instructional program needed to make competency-based education work," said William Spady, the man who set up the Network and director of the National Center for Improvement in Learning. "It's a learning system that can be used to deliver certain goals." The heart of the tie-in between the two concepts, he said, is that both demand that an "assessment-driven system"—a system through which children move by achieving mastery of certain objectives—replace the present "credit-driven system"—a system based on children spending a set amount of time in classes.

"Mastery learning is a square peg in a round hole for most schools," Spady said. "Right now, 'Algebra I' is defined as anything you can get done with your 30 students by the first week in June. Mastery learning implies something totally different, a restructuring of all the brick walls put up by schools—of courses, of credits, of semesters, of 12 years in school and everyone's out."

*   *   *

Looking At Your School:
Tests and Expectations

Running through all the various forms of mastery learning is the matter of tests. It's a confusing subject, much debated and perhaps something to which too much attention is paid.

There are three types of tests commonly used in the public schools—intelligence tests, standardized achievement tests, and criterion-referenced tests. In looking at them, it's important to ask three standard questions: What is being tested? What do the results mean? How will the results be used?

Widespread, formal use of I.Q. tests is waning in the public schools; they've even been abolished in some school systems. However, their results were held for a long time to be indicative of a child's inherent or constant mental ability. I.Q. tests are designed to differentiate among children; they are standardized, norm-referenced tests. The same questions are posed to a large sample of people the same age; those who answer more of the questions correctly are said to be more intelligent than those who get fewer questions right. These tests are constructed to produce a bell-shaped curve with relatively few very smart people at one end, relatively few very stupid people at the other end, and the bulk of the population in the middle. They assume falsely that all people have had the same opportunity to learn what they are measuring—essentially verbal knowledge. And so in schools, they serve little purpose, aside from providing some ready and often damning labels for educators to apply to children, labels of questionable validity. Used as the basis for grouping pupils and then determining the rate and content of instruction, they can be the linchpin of a self-fulfilling prophecy—the "dumb" children learning less because they've been taught less.

Like I.Q. tests, the purpose of standardized achievement tests is to place children along the normal distribution curve. Unlike intelligence tests, the reign of these nationally normed tests is virtually unchallenged. But not only are the scores from these tests difficult for many to understand, they don't provide much information. Standardized achievement test scores typically are reported in terms of grade-equivalents. For instance, the national norm for a test given in the eighth month of the third grade would be 3.8; for a sixth-grade test, given in the eighth month of the school year, the norm would be 6.8. (Again, half of the children fall below the norm and the other half score above it; when one student does well on these tests, somewhere another loses.) These scores are but rough measures. A result of 5.8 for a third grader on a third-grade test may well be cause for parental pride, but it does not mean that the child is doing as well as the average fifth grader; it only means that he is achieving far better than the average third grader in the sample of students used to set the norm for the test. Further, for the child who fares poorly on the test, his score doesn't reveal much about what skills he needs to learn or about the effectiveness of his teachers or the school's programs.

Standardized achievement tests perhaps are most useful in looking at the collective performance of all children in a particular school or system. However, even these collective scores must be considered with great care. Educators are under great pressure to have their pupils succeed on these tests. Outright cheating has occurred in some cities; high test scores also can be the product of excluding certain types of children from taking the tests. It's wise to look at achievement test scores over at least a three-year period, but some large school systems make a regular practice of changing achievement tests every few years. This, of course, prevents firm year-to-year comparisons of the district's programs.

In contrast to intelligence and standardized achievement tests, the third group—criterion-referenced tests—are not designed to elicit 50 percent success and 50 percent failure, do not pit student against student, and can be of great value in diagnosing children's educational needs and in judging the quality of teachers and programs. This type of test carries an entirely different set of expectations, one that does not preclude all children from doing well. These are the tests that drive the mastery learning method.

Instead of being composed of questions designed to differentiate among children, criterion-referenced tests are made up of questions derived directly from what the children are supposed to have learned, the objectives set for each lesson. Their development is begun by clearly specifying what is to be taught in the school's program; test items then are selected to measure students' mastery of these objectives. A common example of a criterion-referenced test is the one that drivers have to take in order to get their licenses. States set clear rules of the road and certain criteria for safe operation of vehicles; prospective drivers get their licenses when they can show they know most of these rules and that they have the necessary driving skills. If they fail the test, they're usually told why—what they don't know or haven't mastered. Almost everyone passes, even if some require much more practice time and have to take the test more than once.

As in the mastery learning strategy, criterion-referenced tests can be a basic part of instructional programs—guiding teachers to what lessons require more study time, allowing the children to set the pace of instruction. These tests can become a charge to schools, a way of focusing otherwise fragmented instructional efforts and evaluating teachers and programs. And since they do not carry the implicit expectation that half (or even some) of the children will fail, they can prompt a drive toward high achievement for all children.

Still, the pitfalls are many. There has to be agreement on educational goals. They have to be stated in clear terms. The tests have to measure mastery of these goals adequately. And last, as a court-appointed team, studying 23 racially isolated schools in San Diego, pointed out in a 1980 report: "No one gains weight just by stepping on the scales." That is, testing of children in itself does not produce learning.

Management systems—with elaborate ways of keeping track of children's progress—are in vogue across the country. Some are said to reflect the principles of mastery learning, but often they're misleading. They do involve criterion-referenced testing, but they do not necessarily involve improving the interaction between children and teachers; they do not necessarily imply high-quality instruction.

Mastery learning—as it was conceptualized by Benjamin Bloom and as it has begun to be put into practice in Chicago, for example—ties testing to direct, explicit instruction. Without that instruction, nothing changes; the kids who need it the most will not have any more of an equal opportunity to learn.

3

The Politics of Reading: *DISTAR*

It was a long, hard struggle for Edna Pettaway. But after four years of dashed hopes and constant worries, she finally got what she wanted more than anything else: Troy, her nine-year-old son, at last had begun to read. "We tried everything," said the middle-class, black housewife. "I was beginning to believe he couldn't learn anything. You know, we party with our friends, and they like to brag about their kids. Well, now I got something to brag about this time: We got the problem licked—he's *reading*."

Troy started kindergarten at a public school in a small town about 25 miles northeast of Houston. At the end of the first grade, he could handle arithmetic adequately, but he couldn't read at all. His teacher suggested something was wrong; perhaps he was retarded. So Mrs. Pettaway took Troy to a psychologist and an eye specialist, only to spend $1000 to find out he was perfectly normal.

She then enrolled him in a highly regarded private school. After a year, he still couldn't read a sentence. When it came time for his reading group, he would become bashful and lie down on the classroom floor. His new teacher said he was just too slow, too shy. In desperation, Mrs. Pettaway sent Troy to one more school: Wesley Elementary, a public school located in a black community called Acres Homes.

Acres Homes is a deeply impoverished, semirural backwater tucked away on the north side of booming Houston, seven miles from the city's prosperous downtown. In the 1930s, it was one of the few places in the Houston area where blacks could own their own homes; city water and sewers were not provided until 1969. A former professor of Mrs. Pettaway's at Texas Southern University had recommended Wesley to her, but she was not impressed with the neighborhood or the vision of the type of children with whom Troy would be attending school. She took one look at the seven-foot-high, chain-link fence guarding Wesley, the tumbledown wooden shacks along Acres Homes' narrow streets, the open drainage ditches swollen with rain water and decided: "There's no way these people are going to be able to help my kid."

But students all around the Wesley School were reading at or above their grade levels; in fact, their test scores were far higher than those at many of Houston's suburban schools. They were speaking clearly and thinking sharply, figuring out problems in elementary logic with enthusiasm and discussing in precise terms subjects like the muscles of the body and the geologic ages of the earth. And Troy came home after one week at Wesley with schoolwork, work he could read. Soon he started picking up the newspaper and reading from the sports pages. Then he started reading with expression. "I can't tell you how I felt," Mrs. Pettaway said. "One day, I just looked at him, sat down and cried. There's something about the reading program at Wesley. Every school should have it. They're doing it, putting it all together. I haven't been able to figure it out yet. It's like magic."

The "magic" at Wesley boils down to its teachers putting a tremendous amount of hard work every day into running their students rapid-fire through a minutely sequenced, highly structured series of reading and language drills. These lessons are part of a commercially available instructional program called DISTAR, a registered trade name short for "Direct Instruction Systems for Teaching and Remediation." Mrs. Pettaway's inability to figure out DISTAR should be pardoned, for the program bears almost nothing in common with the way students are taught in most of America's public schools.

But DISTAR works. It consistently has delivered what other programs usually just promise. Even more convincingly than mastery learning (to which it is related in some ways), it has provided powerful proof that virtually all children can learn. In the largest, most expensive, most ambitious social experiment ever conducted in the United States—in which nine different instructional programs representing the major educational theories of the 1970s were pitted against each other to find out what works best with low-income children—DISTAR far and away came out on top: It was the only program that showed it could bring poor children up to the average achievement levels of their middle-class peers with some regularity—the previously unattainable educational goal of the "War on Poverty."

DISTAR takes the mystery out of teaching kids to read; in the process, it reveals many of the underlying flaws of traditional instruction. Rife with clear cues as to what it is to be learned, intensive student participation, positive reinforcement of the lessons and immediate feedback from the teacher, DISTAR carries Benjamin Bloom's principles of high-quality instruction to their ultimate, systematic conclusion: programmed direct instruction. It leaves nothing to chance. Every action by the teacher—verbal and nonverbal—is specifically outlined; every student response is similarly choreographed. Everywhere it is taught the same way: in small groups, with students and teachers face-to-face in touching range, and with only a flip chart, storybooks, or worksheets between them.

DISTAR lessons are language-rich, quick, and lively. Drill follows drill in short order. Students are awake and participating, more than willingly. There is a palpable rhythm afoot in the classroom, a singular cadence of learning. All the time, there is give-and-take: patterning and rewards, demonstrations and testing. Witness this lesson on the simple, but critical skill of recognizing long vowels as taught by Troy Pettaway's teacher, Mary Ellen Hassett, to ten of her students.

"Let's get ready to read all the words on this page without making a mistake," Ms. Hassett began, looking directly at the children arranged before her in two concentric circles. In one hand she held a flip chart that bore two words, *made* and *mad,* printed in large type. Her other arm was straight out with the palm of her hand vertical, making a "stop" signal. With that hand, she then touched a small ball underneath the beginning of the word *made* and ordered sharply: "Sound it out. Get ready."

"Mmmaaaaade," each child replied in unison as she quickly ran her finger underneath each letter of the word.

"What word?" she fired back, punctuating the question with a loud snap of her fingers as her hand twirled theatrically in the air. "Made," the children responded in harmony. "Yes, made," she repeated. "Good."

Ms. Hassett then touched the small ball underneath the next word *mad* and ordered again: "Sound it out. Get ready."

"Mmmaad," the students read together as she moved her finger underneath the word. "What word?" she asked. Snap!

"Mad," came the chorus. "Yes, mad," Ms. Hassett concluded, having heard not one hesitant voice. "That's good talking. Give yourself some butterfly claps." And the children broke into broad smiles, rapidly fluttering their hands past one another in silent applause.

Each of these two drills was repeated several times in exactly the same fashion until Ms. Hassett put one of her arms out in a "stop" signal and pointed with the other to *a* in the word *mad* on the chart. "Here's a rule," she said. "If there is an *e* on the end of the word, you say the name of this letter. Remember that rule."

Then she pointed to the *a* in *made*. "There's an *e* on the end of this word. So tell me the name of this letter," she ordered. "Get ready." Snap!

"Aaaaa," every child chanted.

"Read this word the fast way and say the name aaaaa," she instructed, pointing again to "made." Pause. "Get ready." Snap!

"Made," the students answered. "What word?" she shot back. "Made," they replied again. "Yes," she reiterated. "Made. Good talking. Give yourselves a pat on the back." And each of the children reached up and proudly patted himself on his shoulder a few times.

These two drills also were repeated again with the students pronouncing the words and Ms. Hassett individually correcting them until she could tell that each firmly knew the difference between the sounds. In just these few minutes, the children had learned an important rule by example. In succeeding lessons, they would learn to apply that same rule in discriminating between such new pairs of words as *rode* and *rod* and *cape* and *cap*. It would be as fast and easy, just as spelled out, and just as regimented, with the same back-and-forth verbal flow, controlling signals, and little room for error. And in teaching this way, Ms. Hassett would not be alone; in Wesley's other primary-grade classrooms, instruction would proceed in exactly the same fashion. Whether the lessons were on opposites:

"This door is . . . ?" asked the teacher, pointing to a picture of a refrigerator with an open door. "Open," her students replied together. "Say the whole thing," she ordered. "The refrigerator door is open," they answered again.

"This door is . . . ?" she then asked, pointing to another picture of a refrigerator with its door closed. "Closed," the students responded at once. "Say the whole thing," she ordered again. "The refrigerator door is closed," they replied again.

Or on reviewing the organization of the human body:

"Watch my signal," the teacher commanded. "Get ready. . . . Femur." The children cried, "Skeletal." And she shot back, "Esophagus." And they cried, "Stomach."

Or on simply reading stories:

". . . We will load the TV sets into the train cars," one student read aloud. "Everyone," his teacher said, "look at me. What will they do?" "They will load the TV sets into the train cars," all the students chanted.

Such repetition, group responding, and precise human engineering—built into each of the hundreds of primary-grade DISTAR lessons in reading, math, and language—rankle most public school educators, who disdainfully have labeled it everything from "the way chimps are trained" to "brain-washing" to the "thalidomide of education." Said one New York City principal: "The technique of DISTAR is so utterly contrary to what teachers have been taught about student-teacher relationships and pedagogy. No conscientious principal or teacher in his right mind would stay in the room more than five minutes before walking out in total disgust."

But at the Wesley School—where, in 1975, some 40 percent of the sixth graders could not read at all—DISTAR has meant no nonreaders and test scores well above the national standards. Instead of sixth graders literally struggling through first-grade readers word by word, it has meant third graders reading everything put before them—with comprehension. It has meant second graders turning around to ask with impeccable pronounciation: "What does this word *peevish* mean?" And it has meant revitalized teachers. "This is a whole new world for me," said Lorraine Killion, a third-grade teacher who used to teach sixth graders. "My 12-year-olds would just sit there. But these kids have the skills to sound out words, to attack them, with no tension, no guessing. We get so much done in a day—it's amazing." Added Jan Austin, the first Wesley teacher to use DISTAR: "It definitely has made a better teacher of me. I'm more aware of how to correct the problems children are having; I don't let anything slide now. Parents are more receptive because their kids can do things at home now."

Some parents, like Mrs. Pettaway, drive up to 60 miles a day so their children can attend Wesley. Many others say if the program were moved from the school, they'd follow DISTAR anywhere. "I didn't think that he could be reading so soon," said Carolyn Lee, whose son is in kindergarten. "But he isn't just associating words and pictures; he's really looking at the words and pronouncing them. I'm not sure I'm ready for all the things he's started thinking and talking about now. But it's so good to see a child that wants to learn, that wants to do his work. It's the program—if the school didn't have it, he would be learning at a much slower pace."

All of this, for one of Wesley's longtime special education teachers, is just "unbelievable, unreal, a true success story." But for Thaddeus Lott, Jr., Wesley's principal, it's simply a matter of it being "much too expensive to ask taxpayers to pay for education they're not getting, for teachers to sit on their behinds, pick up their checks, and not teach kids."

Lott, a stocky black man in his forties, lives in Acres Homes, where he was born and raised. His father was the minister of a local Baptist church; Lott attended and later taught at a nearby elementary school. In the late 1970s, he sent two of his children to Wesley—only to have to pull them out because the school was so bad. When he was named Wesley's principal in 1975, he found the school "a mess." The kids were running wild; there were bloody fights every afternoon on the front lawn; the place was dirty. Lott's a hard worker; he likes to run a tight ship. "I spent that first year getting everything clean and getting some discipline back in here," he said. He also put his staff on a bus one day to travel to Bay City, Texas, where another elementary school was using DISTAR.

Wesley had a "language experience" reading program, one that relied on the children's own vocabulary and tolerated incorrect grammar and mispronounced words. Lott first substituted DISTAR in the lowest achieving first-grade class. The teacher came back after a while and told him she couldn't tell her students from those in the highest ability group because they had begun to read so well. The next year, he tried DISTAR with a class of fourth graders who couldn't even decipher first-grade primers; within three or four weeks, they began to pick up some skills, began to read. Wesley's teachers initially were reluctant to abandon the basal reading program, but there was no question in Lott's mind. Within two years, every primary-grade class at Wesley and some classes of low-achieving upper-grade students were using DISTAR.

"It's the direct contact that makes it work," he said. "It's voice to voice, eye to eye. It teaches to mastery every day. The children hear the sounds. The teachers know right away when a child is bombing out. It's like being able to teach one-to-one in a group. It's so well organized; the teachers have to teach it the way it's supposed to be taught, and they know it. The management—the accountability for attaining education goals—is built right in. It puts the emphasis where it needs to be—on teaching. With DISTAR, you have to work hard. But DISTAR shows us that every kid can learn, if he's taught."

DISTAR's striking success at Wesley led the Houston Independent School District to fund training for about 800 teachers at 60 of its 130 elementary schools. It sent Lott on the road as a spokesman for the program's publishers; and it attracted more than 600 visitors to Wesley in 1979, many of whom went home and adopted the program. But long before Wesley, DISTAR was well on its way toward producing the most impressive record of results in the recent history of this nation's public schools.

For instance, in the Lawndale area on the west side of Chicago, about 6000 children a year were exposed to DISTAR from 1971 to 1976, after District 10 Superintendent Joseph Rosen told his teachers, "You're not doing your jobs." Lawndale is one of the poorest areas in Chicago; DISTAR brought the children—in kindergarten through grade three—to above the citywide average on standardized tests. At one District 10 school, the Burns Branch School where enrollment was 95 percent Hispanic, the 1974 second-grade average reading test score was 3.2 (compared to the national norm of 2.8), according to a report by J. S. Fuerst of Loyola University. At the same time, Fuerst found, DISTAR was taking more economically privileged second graders at the Ogden School, near Chicago's "Gold Coast," to a 4.1 average. "It works with two things—teacher training and supervision," said Rosen. "It's a tough operation—the teachers have got to listen to the kids." (Despite its success, DISTAR's use in District 10 waned after Rosen retired in 1976.)

In Mt. Vernon, New York, the poorest of 40 school districts in affluent Westchester County, student achievement also was at the bottom of the heap in 1971. But by 1980, after nine years of using DISTAR in every one of its schools, the percentage of third graders failing the state competency exams in reading and math dropped from about 37 to about 6 percent; at the sixth-grade level, the failures on these tests fell from about 50 to about 25 percent. In some Mt. Vernon schools, the drop in the percent failing was as much as 60 percentage points; and the district as a whole passed 13 far wealthier Westchester districts in achievement. "We first thought DISTAR was a remedial program," said William Prattella, Mt. Vernon's superintendent. "But then we found that it's the one program applicable to all youngsters; it's good for all SES [socioeconomic statuses], all intelligence levels." Ruth Cafarella, the district's former reading supervisor, credited DISTAR with improving area black schools so much that it "helped end racial turmoil in this city, saved this town." Mt. Vernon is just north of the Bronx. In the early 1970s, blacks were moving in and whites were leaving, fearful of a loss in school quality; by the end of the decade, the tide was reversing as young white families were attracted back by Mt. Vernon's schools. "DISTAR," said Prattella, "is the most significant thing to happen here in 15 years."

And in East St. Louis, Illinois, about 1000 primary-grade students in seven schools racked up test scores a full year above their grade levels in almost every year of the 1970s because of DISTAR. It took the Robinson School, with the poorest students in that blighted, forgotten city, to the highest sixth-grade test scores in town, far above the national norm. "It teaches, brother," said Vera Williams, Robinson's principal. "It really addresses the problem of inadequate teacher education. The teachers don't always like it. But it provides a lot of guidance; they're not just thrown in a classroom and told, 'Here, teach.' We would be hopelessly behind without it. It may not be the one answer. But all I can tell you is, the children around here can read. And everywhere else you see children who can't."

Research on DISTAR shows it has had dramatic effects with almost every kind of child—with the gifted and the socially disadvantaged, the moderately retarded, the severely retarded, the behaviorally disturbed and the dyslectic. Its principles have been successfully applied to teaching new vocabulary to deaf children using high-frequency sound waves received as skin vibrations—essentially an "external ear," the development of which had foiled researchers for more than 40 years. In the 1976 "Follow Through" study of more than 20 communities reflecting a cross-section of low-income America—rural and inner-city blacks, rural whites, Mexican-Americans, native Americans—DISTAR enabled some 8000 students to reach normal achievement levels in the basics by the third grade and show outstanding gains in measures of their pride and self-confidence. It has worked with low-income children in Las Vegas, New Mexico, and in the Ocean Hill–Brownsville section of Brooklyn; in Dayton, Ohio, and Eugene, Oregon; in Tupelo, Mississippi, and San Diego, California. "DISTAR definitely works," said Suzanne Rimes, the Wesley School's program coordinator. "A lot of people don't believe it when they hear it. They don't want to believe it. It's easier to make excuses than really do the job.

"You have to revise your whole way of thinking about children. We've been blaming children for what they couldn't do, but we weren't teaching them before. You don't realize it until someone puts something like this in your hands, and you see it. Now we can look every parent in the eye and guarantee success: We can teach their children to read."

*   *   *

The father and guiding light of DISTAR is a tall powerfully built man in his late forties. He has a salt-and-pepper beard, is given to wearing jeans and motorcycle boots, and speaks his mind at every turn. Siegfried Engelmann's colleagues across the country affectionately refer to him as "Ziggy" and know him as an angry, impatient genius.

In the college town of Eugene, Oregon, Engelmann works in a small, windowless room in the basement of a building housing the "Corp.," the Engelmann-Becker Corp. There is an ancient typewriter in the room, a few books, and enough space for him to gesture with his arms at full length, which he does repeatedly as he makes his points. If he curses and sighs throughout the conversation, it is because after 15 years of developing successful instructional programs that fly in the face of those who control the American education industry, he finds it "deeply affronting that kids can be taught and they're not." And if his voice rises shrilly, it is because he believes the way of traditional education is "bull, complete and utter bull."

"The whole educational establishment from stem to stern is worse than medieval medicine," he says, slapping his hand on his desk. "Administrators don't know what works in the classroom. Teachers don't know how to teach. So the students don't learn. And who gets blamed? The students. That's the whole logic. What percentage of the kids in Cincinnati or anywhere get report cards saying they can't read because they weren't taught right? I'll tell you—zero, none.

"The kids are the problem. They cause the problem. That's 100 percent of the diagnosis. There's no possibility in their minds that the kid is responding perfectly naturally and the problem is with the teaching. The teaching is perfect—that's so foolish, absurd, invalid. They're not teaching; they're presenting material, name calling.

"The schools are designed to produce a high percentage of failure. They're operating under two persistent myths: One, the public schools have done great things with the poor in the past; and two, educators are convinced of their own good will. None of this is true. I've dealt with more than 100 school districts. No one cares about results; none of them are positively motivated to change their programs. You give me a school district and I'll show you no failure kids—zero, none. And no failure teachers, too.

"I'll tell you where educators are at. If a teacher were to go out on the playground and cut a kid's hand off, her principal would claim he didn't know about it, that she's a 'mad woman.' But if he tolerates her day after day raping kids' minds in her class, then she's a 'nice lady.' In every school, there's a teacher like that. Everyone knows who she is; no one does anything about her. Well, I'm sorry, God damn it, she's not a 'nice lady.' "

Engelmann is a heretic in academia. By his own admission, he has a "low tolerance for bullshit. And the higher you go up the ladder of education, the more the bullshit increases to an intolerable degree. Why not call it for what it is? Schools aren't going to make sincere changes in an evolutionary way; they thrive on 'changing.' What's needed is a revolution. And it will happen if parents ever get solid data on the difference between the service they're supposed to get and the service they've received, if they ever find out how badly they've been raped."

Appropriately, Engelmann came to work with children without formal training in education, let alone a doctorate. He studied philosophy—"no certain kind, you name it"—at the University of Illinois. He then worked with an oil-development firm, for auto agencies, as a freelance writer, as the science editor of an encyclopedia, and in advertising. Faced with the task of creating commercials to sell candy to kids while working for a Champaign, Illinois, ad agency, he began to research what causes children to learn.

To his surprise, he found little that was directly helpful in the library. There was the work of the behaviorists, "that didn't explain anything beyond a dog lifting his leg after stimulus—nothing about cognitively related behavior." There was the work of the rationalists, "that tried to explain the logic of how a stimulus causes a response by looking at the so-called properties of the learner, but couldn't predict anything." And there were the linguists—"180 degrees wrong." So he began working on his own with some neighborhood children, teaching them logical thinking games.

About the same time, he read about a University of Illinois professor, Carl Bereiter, who had set up a preschool to try to teach four-year-olds to read. Engelmann made a film of his own efforts, in which his students were solving simple algebraic equations, and showed it to Bereiter, who immediately offered him a job. The now-famous Bereiter-Engelmann preschool was born, along with the instructional methods embodied by DISTAR. Each morning at the preschool, they sat in front of small groups of children working on language and math. And every afternoon, they would brutally analyze what they had done right or wrong. After two years, the dozen or so children, all from economically deprived backgrounds, had gained 25 I.Q. points and were reading at the second-grade level, far better than their older siblings.

Bereiter left the project, and Engelmann then teamed with Wesley Becker, a clinical psychologist interested in applying the behavioral principles of positive reinforcement to classroom learning problems. Always letting the children's responses determine the adequacy of their teaching, Engelmann and Becker developed DISTAR with these underlying principles:

• All children can be taught; teaching failure is not excused. If the student fails, diagnose the teaching history.

• The learning of basic skills is essential to intelligent behavior and should be the main focus of a compensatory education program.

• The disadvantaged tend to be behind in the basic skills;

they must be taught at a faster rate—more in less time—if they are to catch up with their middle-class peers.

• Thinking processes—not just simple letter-sound associations, but more complex operations like understanding absurdities—can be taught first as teacher-led, explicit verbal exercises.

• Teaching programs derive from the nature of the skills and knowledge to be mastered, not the nature of the individual. It is possible to teach all children with the same program sequence.

• Teaching sequences are designed to permit only one interpretation whenever possible. In other words, when DISTAR teaches the color "red," it does so in a way that the student cannot confuse the property "red" with the object "apple," or the class of objects "food," or other descriptive properties "small," "round" or "smooth."

• When the time comes for a student to apply a skill to a different task, this, too, must be planned for in the teaching program and then taught. There is no magic in learning.

More than anything, however, DISTAR is about controlling the details of what happens between students and teachers once the classroom doors are closed. Only in this way can more be taught in less time. And so:

• Aides are used to increase the amount of student-teacher interaction.

• Daily activities are structured carefully with a clear priority on teaching—to reduce wasted time and to increase the amount of time students are engaged in academic activities.

• Rapid-paced, small-group, teacher-directed instruction is specified as the most efficient way to individualize lessons.

• Programs focus on general cases, rather than specific examples. In this way, whole sets of knowledge can be generated from smaller subsets. For example, DISTAR teaches beginning reading systematically with a heavy emphasis on phonics, or the sounds that make up words. It first teaches 40 separate sounds and then the skills for blending them together, imparting quickly a generalized skill to unlock more than half of the commonly used English words.

• Daily lessons are scripted, telling the teacher exactly what to say and do and when to use positive reinforcement—point systems, praise—to strengthen children's motivation.

• Student and teacher progress is monitored through biweekly tests and teacher reports on the number of lessons taught.

• Teachers are provided with extensive training, and are not allowed to deviate from the program. Trained supervisors are expected to spend about three-quarters of their time in classrooms, working with teachers and aides.

DISTAR literally mandates teaching. About two and a half hours a day are required to go through its three programs, about 45 minutes each for reading, math, and language. With the children divided into two or three small groups of no more than ten or twelve students, DISTAR is a school day's work for both a teacher and an aide.

Each of the programs has three levels, generally used in kindergarten through grade three. (There are other programs for older children in "Corrective Reading.") Reading I begins with an intensive focus on phonics; by Reading III, students are reading for content from social studies and science selections. The arithmetic program starts with the basic operations and ends with children performing long division, multiplication, and lengthy word problems. The DISTAR language program, perhaps the most inventive of the three, provides an introduction to the language and concepts of instruction (identity statements, opposites, comparisons, classification, and verb tense, among others) and moves through the properties and relationships of events and objects to Language III, where children learn written and oral sentence structure and logical reasoning skills.

On the surface, DISTAR seems to have a lot in common with mastery learning, particularly the continuous progress/mastery learning program developed in Chicago. Both use scripts, teach to "mastery," and stress direct instruction in whole groups. Most importantly, both share the belief that all children can learn. The research supportive of mastery learning—on student abilities, on expectations, on direct instruction, on academic engaged time, and on the importance of a strong academic focus—applies equally, if not more so, to DISTAR.

However, where mastery learning suggests certain teacher behaviors, DISTAR commands them. Where mastery learning depends on a tight sequence of skills in small steps, DISTAR assumes that kids know next to nothing and so its steps are microscopic, even more carefully patterned. Where mastery learning makes for more actively involved students, DISTAR produces students who are performers like no other. Where mastery learning attempts to equalize the opportunity to learn, DISTAR attempts to insure that each child learns. And although mastery learning and DISTAR are close cousins within the wide scheme of American education, both Engelmann and Michael Katims, the developer of Chicago's mastery learning program, have little respect for each other's efforts.

"In this business, the people who line up next to you are the ones you have to watch out for the most," Engelmann said, referring to mastery learning. "They're usually simple-minded. They don't deliver anything; they're too locked into the system." Engelmann views mastery learning's stress on covert conceptual operations, such as advising students to make "mental pictures" of actions described in reading passages, as too "amateurish," too unspecific. "It's all that metacognitive crap," he said. "Picture this and picture that—there's no way to test whether the kids are really doing it. Mastery learning is a series of school-marmish tasks, developed by a bunch of teachers who took a look at what's on the achievement tests and are trying to teach that."

The critical difference between DISTAR and mastery learning, for Engelmann, is that his program represents a series of "fine discriminations" leading to generalizable skills, whereas the Chicago program relies too heavily on abstract, verbal instructions and concepts for which children are not prepared. While mastery learning leaves a wide berth for error, he says, DISTAR presents "sets of examples that cannot fail to convey that which you're trying to teach."

The ways in which the two programs approach teaching the directions "left" and "right" (an important concept for beginning reading) are illustrative. In mastery learning, children are told: "Some things go in a special direction. We read in a special direction. It's called left to right." But in DISTAR, "left to right" is taught as a relative order, a sequence of events. Before the children learn the two directions, they learn "first" and "then"—through a variety of exercises including learning how to clap and touch their heads in either order on command.

Michael Katims says all this amounts to "answering not thinking, all stimulus and response. It's like what was used on prisoners in the Korean War: DISTAR does what it can to get you to say 'a,' then it goes into a sequence of actions to get you to say 'b' and then it works on getting you to say 'ab'—all the way through the alphabet. The kids are not able to generalize; they're just learning special answers to special questions. It works in the early grades, but what happens later on when the curriculum becomes too diverse, when you can't take into account any longer the realities of little minds? It builds in cognitive limits because it only deals with part of the problem, thereby causing even greater problems."

For Katims, DISTAR is too finely tuned: "DISTAR leaves no gaps. And no learning occurs because of that—the gaps are where learning happens, where the kids make their own connections. DISTAR just provides the blocks; mastery learning kids get both the blocks and the mortar because they're going to have to start building their own walls some day."

Katims's charges are the least of those against DISTAR. Almost everywhere it has been introduced, DISTAR has stirred deep initial opposition. It has been opposed by those who see it as rote learning; by teachers who say it stifles their creativity; by teachers' unions nervous about the increased instructional responsibility given to teachers' aides; by minority people who say it makes the racist assumption that their kids don't know anything because of a language and cultural deficit; by school administrators who say it's too costly, too rigid, and too much trouble ("And anyway," they often add, "no one way works best for all children"); and by the deeply entrenched proponents of unstructured, discovery-oriented, "open" education who view it as manipulation of children, behaviorism gone wild.

"One of the reasons for the reaction is that it requires teachers to work like hell," said Ruth Cafarella, of Mt. Vernon, New York. "If they're not feeling well one day, they're used to resorting to the 'purple passion,' passing out ditto sheets for kids to look busy." When DISTAR was introduced in Mt. Vernon in 1972, she said, "there was a terrible reaction. In some cases, teachers put parents up to protesting, telling them the program was only for poor kids. We had to call in the assistant superintendent to tell the teachers if they wouldn't give DISTAR a try, they could turn in their resignations immediately."

Other reading programs "would provoke the same reaction as DISTAR, if teachers were required to follow them exactly as they're supposed to be done," said Paul Copperman, author of *The Literacy Hoax*. "The difference between DISTAR and all the others is that it can't be used lightly, without training, without watching teachers." Copperman is president of the California-based Institute of Reading Development, which conducts high-level reading classes under contract with schools and corporations using a technique similar to that of DISTAR. "We train our teachers to death," he said. "And then like DISTAR, we expect them to teach and teach and teach."

But the opposition to DISTAR, in many instances, runs far deeper than issues of hard work or extensive training. It stems from the political structure of large school systems' bureaucracies, which have grown dependent on the power and money attached to the scores of federal and state compensatory education programs that frequently have failed to show results.

Some urban school systems operate as many as 60 different compensatory education programs, each with its own outside funding source and mode of instruction. The result often is competition among administrators, fragmented instructional efforts, continual interruptions as children are pulled out of regular classrooms for special services, and dilution of the responsibility of regular classroom teachers. Some inner-city schools receive funds from as many as three dozen of these programs, but their staffs often are hard pressed to identify which kids are in which program. Although the slightest sign of improvement among children often is ballyhooed beyond belief, successful learning doesn't seem to be the real expectation or goal; rather, maintaining the flow of money appears to be an end in itself.

The use of DISTAR, by contrast, has caused some low-income schools to lose their special funding because students began to achieve so well in the program. Its documented successes make lies of many of the underlying assumptions of traditional compensatory education programs: the concept of "readiness for reading"; the practice of pulling low-achieving students out of their regular classes for special instruction (often at a lower level and slower pace); the vogue of labeling children as having "specific learning disabilities." The problem is, American education tends to measure the worth of instructional programs not by their results, but by their agreement with prevailing notions about how children should be taught. And so DISTAR's results have prompted more resentment than interest.

In the early 1970s, for example, Engelmann wanted to leave the University of Illinois to set up a graduate teacher-training program elsewhere. Even though he had projects in hand worth nearly a million dollars a year (that would financially benefit any university), his proposals were rejected by seven schools before the University of Oregon agreed to take him in. At one major university, the staffs of two departments voted unanimously against him coming to their campus.

"The whole world is looking for an answer—and no one wants to admit that DISTAR works," said Lloyd Cooke, who is promoting the use of both DISTAR and mastery learning in the New York City area on behalf of the Economic Development Council. "Everyone who looks at it figures there's something else going on—that the kids are memorizing or that they can't think by themselves. But DISTAR kids can read, are articulate, think before they speak and then talk in complete sentences. The problem with the program is that it violates everything that's been held up as tried and true in education. It requires so much change in educators' behavior that it almost can't succeed in most school systems today."

*   *   *

Nothing shows the depths of the resistance to DISTAR better than the reaction to the results of the federally funded "Follow Through" project.

Follow Through was set up in 1967 to extend the "Head Start" preschool program; at the time, research suggested that Head Start was working but that student gains were lost after the first grade. Originally, Follow Through was to be a service project for some 200,000 low-income, primary-grade students. But President Johnson's request for $120 million was slashed to $14 million by Congress, and so the primary purpose of the program shifted to finding out what educational programs work best for low-income students in the first three grades. In the 1970s, Follow Through grew to become the largest social experiment ever conducted in the United States, involving 75,000 children (about 8000 at a time), 180 communities, an annual budget of about $60 million, and more than 20 different instructional programs. More than $500 million was spent during the project's first decade.

Nine instructional programs were studied most thoroughly:

• DISTAR

• The "open education model" based on the British Infant School in which children are expected to take responsibility for their own learning.

• The "Tucson early education model" which focuses on children's own language and experiences.

• The "cognitively oriented curriculum" which allows

children to make their own choices about what to learn, based on Jean Piaget's development concepts.

• The "responsive education model" which keys in on children's self-esteem.

• The "Bank Street College model" which incorporates the philosophies of Piaget, John Dewey, and Sigmund Freud, using a "language experience" approach to reading.

• The "behavior analysis model" which uses tokens to reinforce learning systematically.

• The "Florida parent education model" which teaches (parents to teach their children.

• The bilingual "language development model," in which materials are presented in Spanish first, then English.

Nine years later, a three-million-dollar study of 9200 Follow Through third-graders who had been in the nine programs for at least three years showed that the highly structured instructional programs were much more successful in raising achievement than those based on the "open classroom" concept. And even though many of the "open" programs attempted to work directly on building children's self-esteem, the structured models also were far more successful in raising students' levels of pride, self-confidence, and sense of responsibility.

DISTAR was the leader in all measures and the only program of the nine in which students approached or exceeded national norms in the basics. DISTAR third graders ended up at the 41st percentile in reading and at about the 50th percentile in math, spelling, and language on a standardized achievement test (with the 50th percentile as the norm). The only other major Follow Through model to bring its students above the 30th percentile in reading and math was the "behavior analysis" program, which also is highly structured. And in comparisons to "control" groups of children not in Follow Through, DISTAR and the "language development model" (again, a structured program) were the only two programs to show generally positive results.

Wesley Becker, Engelmann's colleague in designing DISTAR drew these conclusions from the data:

• Money, good will, and comprehensive services do not necessarily cause gains in achievement. All Follow Through programs had these things to the same degree, and most failed to do the job in the basic skills.

• The popular belief that it is necessary to teach different students in different ways is fiction for the most part. The programs that failed the most were those that stressed individual needs in instruction.

• Similarly, the common assumption that self-directed learning is the only meaningful learning is false. There is no way for children to learn the arbitrary conventions of language without someone teaching them systematically.

• There is a need to get the magic out of learning, such as the assumption that once learning objectives are specified, teachers automatically will induce students to achieve these goals. Programs that stressed "cognitive objectives" fared poorly because they did not have the instructional programming to reach these goals.

• Product-oriented management and teacher-support systems are essential for improving the education of the disadvantaged. The programs that channeled supervisors into helping teachers attain specific goals were most successful overall.

• The learning of basic skills does not occur without students spending "time on task." The most successful models provided extensive training to teachers in efficient time management and specific (direct instruction) methods.

For all the programs, reading comprehension proved to be the most difficult area in which to show results. DISTAR was the only one to show significant gains in comprehension, but its students only reached the 41st percentile. Other studies (in East St. Louis, for example) show that DISTAR students fall off in achievement in later grades, although they still maintain a distinct lead over their peers who haven't had the program. Becker believes that gains in comprehension are so difficult to achieve and then maintain because most "schools are not designed to teach the English language to poor kids, whose parents on the average are less well-versed in knowledge of standard English. Schools are basically designed for white middle-class kids and leave largely to parents the teaching of the most basic building block for intelligent behavior—namely, words and their referents."

What is needed beyond the third grade, Becker believes, are programs that systematically teach vocabulary concepts. The problem in designing these programs is that vocabulary is an "additive set," in which the learning of one element provides little help in learning the next; by contrast, the skill of decoding words can be imparted quickly because it lends itself to the teaching of general rules that apply to all the elements of the set. Nevertheless, Becker and Engelmann in the late 1970s began work on developing a program that would teach a basic high-school vocabulary of 7000 words by means of first teaching a smaller set of morphemes. (Morphemes are the smallest units of meaning into which words can be divided. For example, *helper* can be divided into *help* + *er;* and *recognizable* can be broken down to *re* + *cogn* + *ize* + *able.*) They also were at work on DISTAR writing skills and "general information" programs for the upper elementary grades. All these new programs were still several years away from completion in 1980.

Following the release of the Follow Through study in 1976, DISTAR proponents expected that many school systems would want to adopt their program. But not one large school system ever contacted Engelmann or Becker as a result. The National Institute of Education turned down five of their research proposals in the late 1970s. Far from acting upon their costly, extensive study, U.S. Office of Education administrators buried it beneath a tidal wide of qualifications. It was said to be "flawed"; the different models "weren't implemented equally well"; "local differences were stronger than the programs." So the federal education bureaucracy continued to dole out more than three billion dollars each year to local school districts for low-income, low-achieving students without mandating the use of DISTAR or any other program that had shown it could work. And as of 1980, even with a 30 percent overall budget cutback, all the various Follow Through models continued to be funded equally, irrespective of their results.

"Because there's such a sensitivity—a fear—of anything approaching a national curriculum coming down from the federal government, no one in Follow Through from the start really expected that the government would do anything with the study," said Mary Kennedy, former project director for the 1976 study and now a senior research associate with the Huron Institute of Cambridge, Massachusetts. Ms. Kennedy said the flaws in the study—the difficulties in approximating a rigorously controlled experiment—were known when it was begun, "but it wasn't until the findings came in that the methods were criticized. Even when you correct for the flaws in the study, though, the results turn out exactly the same. There were just a lot of academics and liberals who favored the idea of 'open' education and didn't like it when the structured programs won out and the 'open' models looked bad; that's when the criticisms started. The funny thing is that while the academics are liberal, the families we were serving were conservative. When you talk to them, the first thing they'd say is, 'I want my kid to read and write.'"

To Ms. Kennedy, the failure of Follow Through's administrators to act upon their own study was "neither conspiratorial nor malicious, but a typical mix of politics and incompetence."

But there is another way to view Follow Through. Donna Granat, manager of DISTAR for its publisher, Science Research Associates, Inc., offers this analogy to the field of medicine: "Here they've found the 'cure,' after conducting all these ineffective experiments on children all across the country. And what do they do? They not only won't act on it; they won't even admit it. They won't even go to all those communities around the country where children aren't learning and tell them they've got to stop what they're doing—it doesn't work. It's really very insipid, very ugly, when you think about it."

For Engelmann and Becker, however, Follow Through was but a new version of an old, familiar song. "It's politics," said Becker. "The knowledge is there, the resources. But there's an incredible legacy of bad ideas and untrained people who aren't oriented toward getting the job done with kids." Added Engelmann: "People would rather hold a 'hidden navel' theory of learning: You push a button in the kid's navel and he learns for the rest of his life. There's no big news flash here: The kid will reflect whatever you teach him."

Looking At Your School: Instruction

Teaching children to read well from the start is the most important task of elementary schools. But relying on educators to approach this task correctly can be a great mistake. Many schools continue to employ instructional methods that have been proven ineffective. The staying power of the "look-say" or "whole-word" method of teaching beginning reading is perhaps the most flagrant example of this failure to instruct effectively.

The whole-word approach to reading stresses the meaning of words over the meaning of letters, thinking over decoding, developing a sight vocabulary of familiar words over developing the ability to unlock the pronunciation of unfamiliar words. It fits in with the self-directed, "learning how to learn" activities recommended by advocates of "open" classrooms and with the concept that children have to be developmentally ready to begin reading. Before 1963, no major publisher put out anything but these "Run-Spot-Run" readers.

However, in 1955, Rudolf Flesch touched off what has been called "the great debate" in beginning reading. In his best-seller *Why Johnny Can't Read,* Flesch indicted the nation's public schools for miseducating students by using the look-say method. He said—and more scholarly studies by Jeanne Chall and Robert Dykstra later confirmed—that another approach to beginning reading, founded on phonics, is far superior.

As in DISTAR, systematic phonics first teaches children to associate letters and letter combinations with sounds; it then teaches them how to blend these sounds together to make words. Rather than building up a relatively limited vocabulary of memorized words, it imparts a code by which the pronunciations of the vast majority of the most common words in the English language can be learned. Phonics does not discount the importance of thinking about the meaning of words and sentences; it simply recognizes that decoding is the logical and necessary first step.

With research overwhelming on the side of phonics, most publishers were including more phonics in their basal reading programs by 1970. But reports in 1979 by both Flesch and the Council for Basic Education warned that the whole-word method was still very much alive in the public schools. Flesch declared in *Family Circle* magazine that three out of four schools are not using the phonics-first approach and that most of the new phonics-based reading programs represented an attempt by publishers to lay a "window dressing" of fake phonics over traditional look-say materials. And the Council noted: "Picture clues are still used in decoding words, and in one series we examined, the teacher's manual cautioned against having children sound out unfamiliar words."

The reason that schools have not sincerely adopted the demonstrably effective phonics-first approach and dropped the ineffective whole-word method is simple: Reading is a major and often lucrative cottage industry in American education. At least several hundred universities offer graduate programs in reading instruction; publishers produce a flood of new reading concepts, materials, and programs each year; the two most powerful bodies in the field, the International Reading Association and the National Council of Teachers of English, both claim thousands of members. It's simply good business to maintain, as the IRA did in a November 3, 1979, position statement, that "Differences in learning styles and abilities of children emphasize the need for a variety of approaches to meet those individual needs. No single method or approach nor any one set of instructional materials has been proven to be most effective for all children. . . ."

In the face of this unwillingness to recognize that some instructional methods are more effective than others, what can be done? Engelmann's answer is that textbook publishers and university teacher-training programs will change only when school systems refuse to accept their products, and so the way to begin is to exert pressure at the local school level. For the parents of children having problems, Engelmann, in his 1975 book, *Your Child Can Succeed,* offered this advice on how to exert that pressure to force schools to provide effective instruction:

1. Talk with the teacher and find out "what the problem is, what the teacher is doing to correct it, and what reasons the teacher has for supposing that the solution will work." Tell the teacher you expect a remedy that directly addresses the skills in which the child is weak; reject any notions of "readiness" or labels such as "learning disabled."

2. Observe some classes to document management problems, children failing to grasp one lesson before the teacher moves on to the next, and any activities that don't bear directly on the subject of the lesson.

3. Meet with the principal alone. Ask his opinion of the teacher; then ask him to support his opinion with test data on the performance of students in the teacher's classes. Find out the principal's explanation for the activities observed in the classroom, how this instruction relates to the school's policies, what kind of monitoring the teacher receives, and if there is anyone in the school district who is supposed to identify teachers' problems and help solve them.

4. Publicly appeal to the school board on three counts: "The teacher is not dealing directly with the problem; the principal is not actually aware of what goes on in the classroom; and the various supervisors have provided no help to the teacher in becoming more effective."

Engelmann recommended these steps with the optimistic premise that if the school board did not attempt to solve the problem, the parent would have solid grounds for initiating a lawsuit, alleging "educational malpractice." The charge of malpractice as it applies to education would be the same as in other fields: a claim of dereliction of professional duty resulting in injury to the recipient of the services. But within five years after he wrote his book, there were about a half-dozen attempts at pursuing such suits, all of which failed in court.

The most well known of these was *Peter W. v. San Francisco Unified School District* (1976), in which an 18-year-old high school graduate with a fifth-grade reading level alleged that the school district acted negligently in failing to diagnose his reading problems, in assigning him to inappropriate classes with unqualified instructors, and in misrepresenting his achievement by promoting him through 12 years of school and allowing him to graduate with less than an eighth-grade reading level. In ruling on the case, the California state court noted that if it were to hold the school district accountable for students' achievement, it would expose the public schools to "claims—real or imagined—of disaffected students and parents in countless numbers . . . the ultimate consequence, in terms of public time and money would burden them—beyond calculation." And so the court decided (and other courts have similarly concluded) that negligence in education—proving a breach of professional duty—is not possible when the field itself is so ill-defined, when "experts" could be brought in to testify as to the worth of any technique or method.

The lessons of DISTAR, then, are mixed.

The good news is that some methods—as exemplified by the phonics-first, programmed, direct-instruction approach—have been shown to work far better than others.

The bad news is that educators have shown little interest in using these programs and the courts, at least, have refused to hold them accountable for this choice.

4

The Principal Is The Key:
Garrison School

I am in earnest. I will not equivocate. I will not excuse. I will not retreat a single inch; and I will be heard!

William Lloyd Garrison

For more than 80 years, the Garrison School has served the families living in the apartments along the Grand Concourse Boulevard in New York City's South Bronx. As far back as anyone can remember, the brick and limestone "Castle on the Concourse" has always been a place of learning, a good public school. It is the American Dream.

First, it educated the sons and daughters of the Irish, Italian, German, and Jewish immigrants who had left the tenements of the Lower East Side and East Harlem for a flat on the Concourse, a sign of their upward mobility. Then, as this burgeoning middle class followed the freeways and GI loans to suburbia, another wave of immigrants flocked to the eight- to ten-story, Art Deco-style buildings on both sides of the busy, four-lane thoroughfare. And the colors of the children at the Garrison School began to change.

These new immigrants—blacks from the South and Puerto Ricans fleeing the rural poverty of their homeland—sought the same symbols of success as those who came before them. But all through the South Bronx, a cancer took hold. Industry left with tens of thousands of jobs, and depression-level unemployment set in. The welfare rolls overflowed with a third of the population. And the fires burned—50 or more a day, thousands a year, many intentionally set in buildings far too unprofitable to keep up.

The arson-scarred, crime-ridden 20 square miles of the South Bronx became an international symbol of urban devastation: 600,000 people (about the same number as in the entire city of Boston) relegated to life amid hundreds of acres of rubble, a scene so bombed-out that it has served as a convincing backdrop for war movies. The homicide rate soared to more than twice the city's average; so did the level of drug dependency; and so did the number of births with inadequate health care. President Carter came to Charlotte Street in the South Bronx in October 1977 and left pledging to do all in his power to help. Several multimillion-dollar housing projects were proposed, and then rejected. Republican presidential candidate Ronald Reagan visited the same bleak site in 1980; a "People's Convention" was held there that year; a delegation from the Soviet Union was brought in and local politicians asked for $5 billion in foreign aid. "Broken Promises," proclaimed a huge sign flapping nearby on the side of a building's shell.

Everywhere there remains grim poverty, and the violence, drugs, poor health, and bad schools that go with it. Everything has changed from the not too distant past when "the Bronx was beautiful," when living there meant hope. Everything, that is, except the Garrison School. It is a place still dedicated to education, where all around schools have become depressing factories of failure.

The buildings across the Concourse from Garrison are decaying; their storefronts are covered by steel curtains. A fire took the tenement on the corner. A car that broke down one day is stripped completely by the next. The closest most white New Yorkers get to the school is Yankee Stadium, a few blocks north. More than half of Garrison's students are Hispanic—"Nuyoricans," as they are called; the rest are black. Some come to school speaking no English at all. At least a third will not be there the entire school year. All are poor enough to receive free lunches. Many have been educated early into a harsh life. But student achievement has always been high at Garrison, and it remains so.

The school's students read better than their grade level when they leave for junior high. Every year in the 1970s, Garrison was the only school in its district meeting or exceeding national achievement standards; most of the other 16 elementaries in South Bronx's District 7 fell in the lower 20 percent. "The difference between Garrison and all the others," said one school board member, "is like day and night."

Garrision is the rare type of school that educational researchers have come to label as mavericks or outliers: low-income neighborhood schools with exceptionally high student achievement, mirroring that typically associated with schools in middle-class areas. As one teacher put it: "It's the type of school that breaks up all the stereotypes about children from low-income families." There may be two or three other schools like Garrison in New York City. By one estimate, there are perhaps only a couple of dozen in the whole country. Many large urban school systems cannot boast a single example.

Maverick schools are important because they violate the widely held view that schools cannot make much of a difference in the lives of disadvantaged youth, that variations in student achievement largely reflect pupils' family backgrounds. This pessimism about the capabilities of inner-city schools traces back to James Coleman's extensive 1966 *Equality of Educational Opportunity* survey, which concluded: ". . . schools bring little influence on a child's achievement that is independent of his background and general social context." And it runs deep in the minds of those who control America's public schools—from the Boston school committee member who said in the 1960s, "We don't have inferior schools; we've been getting inferior students," to the Cincinnati school superintendent who in the late 1970s excused his system's test scores by noting that "a third of our students are on welfare."

Garrison, though, does not conform to Professor Coleman's statistical thesis. "This school never really changed even though our pupils changed," said Helene Bergman, who's taught at Garrison for 19 years. "The teachers could have developed an attitude that the children were worthless, nothing. The societal problems are certainly there; it would have been easy to give up. But the expectations and levels of teacher involvement never really changed. Children here are somebody; we know they can succeed. This is a middle-class kind of school that happens to have low-income children."

Every child and every adult at Garrison spends the first 15 minutes of each school day silently reading; visitors are handed a newspaper or book during this period. Every teacher is a reading instructor at one time or another during the day. Their students are exposed to a smorgasbord of instructional approaches. For reading, they group and re-group, change classes, and move up and down the five floors of the school according to a schedule so complex it would do justice to a college registrar. Reading groups are held in the school's stairwells, on its atticlike top floor, anywhere there's space. The result is that children who fall behind get up to three hours of reading a day, often in classes of fewer than 15 students.

Those who show signs of excelling are placed in a special program. In that program, a quarter of Garrison's 900 students—mostly from the school's immediate neighborhood—are exposed to such diverse topics as art history, anthropology, drama, ecology, and meteorology. Some prepare for and pass the exam to enter the prestigious high school run by Hunter College. "Teachers here sit with you and help you with your homework problems," said 11-year-old Aileen Rivera, who's in the special program. "They care about their responsibilities." Her friend Kim Velez chimed in: "In other schools, they don't teach you. You do what you want to do, and they let you pass. In this school, if you don't learn, they put you back. They give you more here. They give you discipline and let you have fun. At other schools, nothing is fun. If you have to learn something there, you don't want to learn it; it just goes in one ear and out the other."

Added Michael Johnson, another 11-year-old: "My mother says, '*This* is a school.' "

With such testimony, Garrison in 1979 became the first public elementary school in New York state to receive accreditation from the Middle States Association of Colleges and Schools—an honor certifying that the school meets high standards. The association's visiting committee was so moved that it suggested replacing the cliché, "If we can put a man on the moon, then we can . . . ," with "If the people at Garrision can cause learning to take place, then it can be done anywhere." And it reported: "The faculty and leadership . . . have literally instituted every possible program or project which has promise of being helpful in causing learning. . . . The pupils are continually challenged. . . . The staff appears to make the assumption that each and every pupil can and must and will learn. The children sense this confidence in them and they tend to perform accordingly, confirming the teachers' beliefs. . . . Some observers might take a superficial look at the designs for learning at (Garrison) and call it hodge-podge. . . . [But it is] a remarkable, interlocking set of programs . . . that is impossible to imagine until one sees it in operation. It may appear a bit frenetic at times but the results are incontrovertible."

Said Norman Miller, dean of graduate studies at Pennsylvania's Beaver College and chairman of the visiting committee: "Garrison is so amazing. It's not the building or anything like that; it's the people in it, and their system. There's no question that Garrison proves that many other schools could be doing a much better job. Garrison is what schools can be. And, of course, Carol Russo is at the heart of it, the focus of it all. Anywhere across the nation where kids are learning, you always find a principal like Mrs. Russo.

"She's not about to let the ghetto take over that school. It's *her* school."

* * *

Carol Russo is sitting in her car on a grim side street. A parking lot packed with U-Haul trailers is on one side, Garrison looms on the other, and a Consolidated Edison service center is behind her. Inside the aged, hulking elementary, her students move quickly to group reading sessions, reading labs, gifted and bilingual programs—all according to her "work plan." Down the block and across the clogged lanes of the Grand Concourse, workmen rip apart a six-story tenement gutted by fire a few days back—because she knew who to lean on, and did so unhesitatingly.

Mrs. Russo rubs a spot on the back of her neck that has been hurting since a staff meeting earlier in the day and begins to speak with characteristic intensity. "You have to do it yourself," she says. "That's what it means to be a principal—there's no one around to tell you what to do. Sure, you have to be an instructional leader, but you can't ignore what's happening in your community, what's happening to your kids out there.

"You have to be a political animal."

The South Bronx is more than impoverished; it is a pressure cooker of poverty heated by political flames from every direction. And Mrs. Russo, by all accounts, is a consummate politician. She not only won't let the "ghetto take over" her school, she won't let the creeping cancer come anywhere near. If there's a fire on Walton Avenue, she's on the phone to the borough president's office the next day; then she's talking to parents about organizing to rebuild their homes. "No one gets away with anything around here," says a community worker. "She gets into it immediately." If Garrison holds a graduation ceremony, congressmen, state senators, assemblymen show up. If there's a teacher she wants to hire, she makes calls; if she wants to get rid of one, she makes more calls—even if it means taking on the teachers' all-powerful federation. She has to deal with the health department, the welfare department, the police—not to mention her community school board. There are kids who haven't had enough to eat, whose mothers are dealing drugs, who don't have anywhere to live, who have seen just about everything.

"Russo is totally ready," says a long-time Garrison teacher. "When you're a New York City school administrator, all you can do is react, you don't have time to pro-act. She is trying to do the present and the future all at once—that's why her neck hurts her. This school has been renovated something like 12 times since I've been here. Why is it? Most of the others are a mess. If she didn't have strong feelings about it, it probably wouldn't even be here any more. It takes a whole lot of political involvement. Other principals avoid it as a problem; she's not afraid of it."

Carol Russo has spent almost her entire life at the Garrison School. The daughter of an Italian immigrant, she grew up nearby in an apartment on Morris Avenue, a street blessed by Pope John Paul II when he went to visit New York City's poor in 1979. She recalls her own childhood as being marked by poverty, too. "It was difficult," she says. "I was always going to school with children who were wealthier." She attended Garrison when Lawrence Kelly was the school's principal. Kelly, an early "progressive" educator, "was too easygoing to survive in this day and age," she says. But she looked up to him. He transferred her to an accelerated class. He kept in touch with her through high school and wrote to her when she went away to Hunter College to study French and Latin. In 1952, she felt "impelled to come back and work under him" as a student teacher.

Mrs. Russo's been at Garrison ever since, as a teacher, a "master teacher," assistant principal for four years, and principal since 1970. And all the while she never forgot the lessons Kelly taught her. "He was a principal who got personally involved in his school—not like a lot of others," she says. "He had a philosophy and a subtle way of demonstrating it by going into classes and working with children. The thing I learned from him is how important it is in working with people to use their talents.

"Teachers are human beings. You can't dictate to them, but you can't allow chaos in the guise of democracy. You have to have their respect, but you can't get that by sending flowers. You have to earn their respect. My job is to set and control the direction of the educational program at the school. You can't do that if you don't understand your people. You can't do that if you don't understand all the different levels."

At 48, Mrs. Russo is a tall, stylish woman who has mastered every level of her school. She is an 18-hour-a-day workaholic, intensely committed to extending Garrison's tradition of excellence. She's constantly reading, looking for new ideas and programs. During summer vacations, she's in her office three or four days a week, working on plans for the coming school year. Nothing escapes her attention. "Look, aren't they beautiful," she says marveling at the bas-relief details on the outside of her school. Garrison, she adds, is "my baby." She speaks rapidly, constantly digressing. She can be impatient, her eyes assuming a nervous cast. In the words of her school's namesake, she is in earnest; she will not equivocate, nor excuse, nor retreat; and she will be heard. "She's hyper, but good hyper," says Ron Eberlein, a math teacher and Garrison's United Federation of Teachers representative. "She anticipates problems. She fights for teachers and programs. It's not my disposition to give glowing reports on the schools, but I think she's the greatest."

By the same token, Eberlein adds: "If you're coming here to find a panacea, it doesn't work like that. It's the system— the system that works here—though she's very much that system."

Mrs. Russo's system—along with the teachers she has attracted and nurtured to work within it—is ever evolving. She begins developing her work plan months before the school year begins. Her top teachers are consulted, and administrative chores are farmed out. Schoolwide committees meet to hash out programs. Certain students are matched with particular teachers. There's a lot of talk—"Too much, too much talk," says Mrs. Russo. "Sometimes it drives me crazy." The result is a thick stack of precise plans and Garrison's master schedule—two full pages for each day of the week, detailing hour by hour where the gifted and bilingual programs are meeting, which classes are in group reading, who's in reading lab, who's getting extra work in reading, writing, and math.

Garrison offers an encyclopedic range of programs, services, and instructional approaches: self-contained classes, small-group instruction, nongraded bilingual classes, remedial math, remedial reading, English as a second language, the special program for the "gifted," a math "resource center," interest and talent groups. For group reading, Garrison's students cross grade and class lines to form small clusters with almost every available teacher. When they go to reading lab, their regular teacher joins them so she can reinforce the lessons back in her class. Every teacher has her own reading plan with assignments for each of several small groups within her class. All of this—the movement, the sheer number of programs—is staggering. Combined with a labyrinthine interior such as that at Garrison, it surely would spell chaos and wasted academic time at most other schools. But here it means that each of the children essentially receives a specifically tailored education (even though Garrison has about the same size staff as nearby schools). And it works because all of the disparate elements are purposeful and fused together by frequent testing, a lot of communication, and Mrs. Russo's planning and will. "Structure," she says. "It's very, very important."

Garrison is a textbook example of what modern organization theorists call "client-centered" delivery of services: a network of diverse programs and personnel focused on students under Mrs. Russo's leadership. Like thousands of other urban elementary schools across the country, it receives funds not only from its local school board, but also from a seemingly never-ending list of state and federal programs. At Garrison, these additional resources and personnel are assimilated within a single framework and directed toward schoolwide goals, with a measurable impact on student achievement. At many other schools, however, these extra resources (amounting to billions of dollars each year nationally) often don't make much of a difference in student achievement. A national study, released in 1979 by the National Association of Elementary School Principals, found that more than 60 percent of the principals surveyed said their students receive less benefit from federal funds than from locally funded programs; about 45 percent said waste of this money is much greater, too. One common reason is that these programs, with their separate purposes and funding sources, tend to promote "professional-centered" delivery of services characterized by:

• The practice of pulling children out of their regular classes for special programs (as is done with about 80 percent of the students in the federal Title I program for low-achieving, low-income students). This, quite often, leads to lost instructional time—the very thing which these students need the most. For instance, the 1979 Austin, Texas, school system study, in which administrators discovered that less than half of the school day was devoted to instruction in their schools, also found that students enrolled in more than one compensatory education program were logging even less instructional time than the average pupil in regular programs.

• Maintenance of separate professional identities among personnel. The result is that they often work at cross purposes. "Aides, tutors, and remedial specialists can all increase the total effectiveness of a program, if they are coordinated . . . ," a 1979 University of Delaware study of exceptional schools concluded. "But an army of extra classroom personnel can also interfere with instruction if they are not properly managed."

• Lack of coordination of instructional programs, leading to a patchwork of confusing and ineffective school experiences for the child. Many programs are doing "more harm than good [because of] a welter of restrictive laws and regulations that makes coordination of remedial programs with the regular instructional program very difficult," a 1979 study of specially funded programs in New York City's schools found. "When special programs are placed in a school, they often are not included within the overall school organization, but rather are placed as appendages outside the school's framework, and have little influence on the schooling process."

Garrison was one of ten New York City elementaries examined in this study, and it was the only one in which researchers found formal efforts to coordinate instruction among all the various special programs. Lee Ann Truesdell, a City University of New York researcher who conducted the study, believes Garrison is not just "exceptional for New York City, but also nationally." And she fully credits Carol Russo: "I don't think people realize how terrific she is; she takes everything seriously to the nth degree. The key ingredient is the way she distributes her resources—human beings and time, not money and books. She is very demanding; she has established a norm in that building. She could do as well in a cave with a lump of charcoal."

It would seem to be just that simple, but there are days when Mrs. Russo would no doubt opt for that cave rather than the caldron of poverty in which Garrison sits. "Do you realize how brutal the societal forces are out there?" she asks, gripping the steering wheel of her car. She looks down the street toward the workmen dismantling the gutted building across from Garrison. She looks over at the mothers collecting outside of the school's entrance, waiting to walk their children home. And then she closes her eyes for a moment. "It's amazing that kids can come to school and leave any of this behind. Schools can make a difference—I've seen it. But let's face it: Those forces out there are so hard to battle.

"When I think about the schools where I live in Scarsdale (in affluent Westchester County) and all their money and what they do ... Ugh! It's sickening! How little they do with what they have."

Sometimes Mrs. Russo thinks about leaving Garrison and

the South Bronx. There have been more than a few job offers in recent years—some for as much as $10,000 a year more than she's making. She considers them, but always decides: "I still want to see how much further we can go here. . . . Maybe if I could find someone to take over the school . . . or maybe if I wanted to retire.

"But what would I do if I retired?" she laughs. "I'd probably just get another job—in education."

* * *

More than anything, the story of the Garrison School and Carol Russo illustrates one of the few clear truths on the path toward effective urban schools: The principal's leadership is critical. It is one of those rare axioms that almost everyone involved with schools seems to agree upon. All across the country it echoes.

"I'll tell you one thing," said a Louisville, Kentucky, community organizer, leaning across her table to make the point. "A principal makes or breaks a school."

Said Dennis Gray, associate director of the Council for Basic Education in Washington, D.C.: "Name a good principal, and quality will follow."

Quoting a U.S. Senate select committee on education report, Jim Enochs, assistant superintendent of the Modesto, California, school system, wrote: "If a school . . . has a reputation for excellence in teaching, if students are performing to the best of their ability, one can almost point to the principal's leadership as the key to success."

"The only way around the primacy of the principal's role," said Lawrence Lezotte, a Michigan State University researcher, "is if there's a cadre of teachers who set a high standard for the school. But, of course, you usually don't find that core group unless they've been attracted to the school by a special kind of principal."

Even those involved with such highly structured programs as DISTAR and mastery learning—programs that leave little to chance—say the same thing: They first have to have the backing and understanding of a school's principal before their instructional efforts can succeed. Both programs demand that principals serve as teacher trainers and monitors of instruction. "There has to be a strong arm for the program to work," said Siegfried Engelmann, DISTAR's creator. "You've got to have a quality-control inspector."

It, then, is not surprising that comprehensive studies of maverick schools in the 1970s in New York, Michigan, Maryland, Delaware, Pennsylvania, California, and the Midwest all begin their analyses with "as the principal goes, so goes the school." The consensus is even more broadly shared than that: A 1979 University of Indiana review of 59 case studies of exceptionally successful urban schools (most conducted between 1971 and 1974) found that the most frequently reported variable was the leadership style of the school's principal. As one researcher not so jokingly put it: "Everyone's going for the 'great man' theory of education."

Specifically, these studies say effective principals:

• Take strong initiative in identifying and articulating goals and priorities for their schools. They run their schools, rather than allowing them to operate by force of habit. They hold themselves and their staff members personally accountable for student achievement in the basic skills. They will not accept excuses, however sympathetic they may be to students' problems.

• Understand the school's educational program inside out. They are "instructional leaders" versus "administrative leaders." They often have strong backgrounds in reading instruction, or they have found someone else who can provide direction in this area. Their first priority is instruction, and they communicate this to their staffs.

• Spend about half their time in the school's halls and classrooms. They are not afraid of working directly with

teachers nor of taking over classes to demonstrate more effective teaching techniques. They are "high visibility"
leaders, rather than ones who spend most of their time in
their offices. They might not be aware of everything that's
going on in their schools at all times, but they have created
that impression in the minds of their staff and students.

• Care more about their schools' academic progress than
human relations or informal, collegial relationships with
their staff members. They are not afraid to be disliked.

• Attempt to handpick their staffs despite constraints from
teachers' unions and school system bureaucracies. They put
direct pressure on incompetent teachers to leave, and they
find ways to award excellent teachers with greater responsibilities and recognition. Their message is: "This is the
way we do things here; if you don't agree with it, don't stay
for you're not going to be happy."

• Set a consistent tone of high expectations for their staffs
and their students. This works both ways: what staff and
students can expect from the principal and what the principal expects from them. These principals most likely are
assertive disciplinarians, creating a school climate in which
instruction can flourish.

These characteristics of effective principals describe a set
of professional behaviors, rather than any single type of
individual. "Good principals are watchdogs, rather than
paperwork people," said George Weber, who conducted
one of the first studies on urban maverick schools when he
was with the Council for Basic Education. "They discover
problems and then demonstrate that they can be solved."
Carol Russo, with her intense style, fills the bill, as does
Roger Haynes, a low-key, playful man who has led the
Washington Park Elementary in one of Cincinnati's worst
inner-city neighborhoods to impressive achievement gains
in the late 1970s.

Like many of his students, Haynes is Appalachian, having

grown up in eastern Kentucky. He is personable and streetwise, warm and at times egotistical. As the principal of a high-achieving, middle-class elementary, he was unhappy; he asked to be transferred to Washington Park, where three-quarters of the pupils receive free lunches, where more than half the students move in or out during each school year, and where their average achievement test score hovered at the 10th percentile. Once there, Haynes began telling everyone, "The 'Big WP' is going to be Number One." And with the school's achievement average shooting to above the 30th percentile in his first three years, staff and students alike began to believe it.

Haynes is a hustler, a salesman, a leader—rather than an administrator. "There's a lot that prevents teachers from teaching and principals from 'principaling,' " he said, waving yet another time-consuming form sent out from the district's headquarters. "But my priorities are to support my teachers and to get to know my kids." Haynes cajoles central office administrators to get just those teachers he wants. He spends three hours each day on duty in the school's lunchroom and on its playground; after school, he's on the corner, reminding students to take home their books. A voracious reader, he goes on a closed-circuit TV system— created with money hustled from local foundations—and talks to his students about books. He's started a four-week "academic excellence" summer school for 200 of his top students, again with donated funds. "Everyone wants to come to Washington Park," said one of his teachers. "Haynes is a winner, and everyone wants to go with a winner. He's been a teacher; he knows what it's like to be in the heat of the battle. Just walk through our halls; you can see teaching, hear teaching, and even feel teaching from the time the students enter the classroom until the second they leave."

Carol Russo and Roger Haynes are a rare breed in American education: risk-takers, unafraid of rocking the boat, personally inspiring. There, of course, have been others like them: legendary figures like Seymour Gang, who in the 1960s did away with all remedial classes at Harlem's P.S. 192 and brought his students to a year above national achievement standards; or tough-minded Paul Adams, who in the 1970s turned around the last remaining Catholic secondary school on Chicago's west side, ridding it of gangs and drugs to the point where 85 percent of his students went on to college; or Robert Schain of Wingate High in Brooklyn, who turned the same trick in the late 1970s by infusing every classroom in his school with reading lessons. As economist Thomas Sowell wrote in his 1976 study of black schools known for their excellence, some of these principals "were of heroic dimensions . . . and others were simply dedicated educators." Whatever the case, the key question is how to get more of these leaders as headmasters of the nation's public schools.

The depth of this problem is revealed by the National Association of Elementary School Principals' 1979 study of 1600 of its members. According to that study, the typical head of an elementary school is a 46-year-old white man, married, with ten years experience on his job, a masters degree, and politically conservative views. Rather than portraying a group of risk-takers, the study profiles a profession whose members seem comfortable with the status quo and are under little pressure to change:

• Contrary to almost every other national study, the typical principal reports "his school is having no trouble with declining scores on standardized achievement tests." More than 80 percent said elementary school children are learning more or about the same as ten years ago.

• More than 70 percent of the principals said they feel "very secure" and had no worries about losing their jobs; another 24 percent said they feel "fairly secure." Less than 3 percent feel "somewhat" or "very insecure."

• One in five principals said their performance is rarely or never evaluated; another 10 percent said they're evaluated only once every two or three years. Of those principals who are evaluated formally, the school district's superintendent is the prime or only evaluator more than 60 percent of the time; by contrast, parents participate in only 2 percent of the principals' evaluations.

• More than 80 percent claimed "primary responsibility" for instructional improvement at their schools, but only a quarter said they have much influence on districtwide decisions about elementary education affecting their schools. Their single greatest problem is "dismissing incompetent staff," but only a quarter of the principals of urban schools said they have a say in selecting teachers even in cooperation with central office administrators.

• More than 18 percent of the principals have not had one day of teaching experience in an elementary school; another 4 percent have had less than one year's experience. About one in four was an athletic coach before becoming a principal. Less than half said they would choose to become a principal, if they were starting over again; almost half do not look upon their present job as their final career goal (with the most desired positions being central office supervisor, assistant superintendent and superintendent).

This is not an encouraging picture, but one fraught with clues to the sources of many of the problems of the public schools. "The principal's job is to help create a curriculum that works and see that it's followed through," said education critic Paul Copperman. "Most principals don't get where they are because they're interested in assuming that responsibility; and when they get there, most don't know what they're supposed to do." Added Siegfried Engelmann: "Most principals would rather play mental masturbation games than respond to instructional problems."

Jim Enochs, in Modesto, California, is only slightly more

generous in his assessment of the 31 principals he supervises, dividing them into three types: "Thoroughbreds—the runners and jumpers who you never have to use the whip on"; "plowhorses—you get them all harnessed up, take them out to the field and face them in the right direction, and promise them they can quit at five o'clock, and they'll pull for you"; and "donkeys—you got to pull'em and push'em and kick'em in their butt, and all the time they're braying and trying shift their load." As elsewhere, the "donkeys" outnumber the "thoroughbreds" in Modesto, Enochs admitted. "You put 'instructional leader' in their job description and it's a big 'hardy-har-har.' If the guy isn't a leader, there's not a lot you can do about it. You can't put guts in a guy or make him articulate."

But others take the more hopeful view that the set of qualities embodied by the relatively few effective principals can serve as guidelines in reshaping a great many of their ineffective colleagues. For example, Ron Edmonds, senior assistant to the chancellor of the New York City schools and a Harvard University researcher, believes all the characteristics associated with the exceptional urban schools he's studied can be used as a blueprint to revitalize other schools in need of improvement. His formula for success includes not only strong leadership, but also clearly understood instructional objectives, an orderly school climate, high expectations, and frequent monitoring of student progress (all of which usually stem from the actions of a strong leader). In 1979, he began to apply this formula to about 10 specially selected New York City elementaries, assigning to each a liaison who was to serve as a staff trainer and as a role model for the principal. (Projects along similar lines also were started in Pontiac, Michigan, and Milwaukee about the same time.)

Carol Russo, who was asked to join Edmonds's project but turned the offer down, is both optimistic and pessimistic about the possibility of replicating Garrison's success elsewhere. "I'm not so sure you could bring our system to other schools," she said. "It's the particular people here; this just happens to be right for us." However, she has begun working with three other District 7 principals in an attempt to aid them in improving their schools. "These three are good pupils—they're willing to listen," she said. "Certain others, though, would not be receptive. They'd have to change their philosophies first. They're afraid of that. They don't know enough to be able to get into redesigning their reading programs. They're scared they wouldn't be able to handle it."

Even though she's encouraged Mrs. Russo to work with a few other principals, District 7 Superintendent Carmen Rodriguez believes that singling out certain successful principals as role models for the others to follow can have adverse effects. "It just stirs up resentment," she said. "You really can't guide a principal anyway; each brings a unique flavor to a situation. Their styles can't be copied." District 7 community school board members agreed with their superintendent. They could use every principal of Mrs. Russo's caliber they could find, but at the same time they seem at a loss for what to do with her, except to leave her alone. "You can't mandate the type of involvement at Garrision," said one member, Errol Toulon. "Garrison is our flower; we just try to water it now and then, and not tamper with it. Any others have to be developed from the ground up. This is a rose in the forest, so we leave the soil underneath it alone."

Looking At Your School: The Principal

Accountability is the rising cry in public education. By 1980, 38 states required students to take "competency" exams. At the same time, some 20 states had approved or were considering proposals requiring teachers to pass their own set of exams in order to be hired, and some school systems were beginning to tie evaluation of teacher performance more closely to students' achievement. But even with the nearly unanimous recognition that school principals have an overwhelming influence on whether their students learn, no state had adopted competency standards for its principals, and some still lacked basic certification standards. Apparently, accountability remains a good idea for those in the classroom but not for those whose job it is to lead the entire enterprise.

Even in communities where parents have won some influence in selecting and evaluating principals, many of the traditional practices persist. Principals tend to be chosen on the basis of seniority and political ties; they tend to be evaluated on the basis of their adult charms—how adroit they are at public relations. All of this misses the point, of course. If improvement in student achievement is the desired end, the principal's ability to provide instructional leadership is the critical question. And it should be asked every step along the way.

Selection

Surprisingly, many school districts do not even specify in their job descriptions that they expect principals to serve as instructional leaders. Aware of the research relating the principal's role to students' academic performance, David Schiering, a Cincinnati school board member, was shocked to discover in 1980 that his board's policy basically defined the principal as a "school building administrator." He responded by suggesting that those selecting principals— students, teachers, parents and administrators, in this case—should do more than just interview candidates and recommend a choice; they also should set specific educational goals for their school and find a leader with corresponding qualifications, who then can be held accountable for reaching these goals.

Nat Hentoff, a New York City journalist, had some more suggestions for selecting principals in a Jan. 15, 1979 *Village Voice* article: It "ought to be done the way a reporter approaches a complex story: extensive interviews with students and faculty in the schools where the applicant worked, and a careful canvassing of the surrrounding communities. . . . Was he a clock-watcher, or the kind of educator who stayed as long as each day's crises and conundrums required? And, of course, how well did the kids he taught or supervised do after they left his school?"

Training

Most in-service training for administrators is about as bad as that which is foisted upon teachers; it usually bears little relationship to what matters in the classroom, is seldom applied, and simply amounts to fulfilling pro forma requirements. By contrast, programs that take instruction seriously—such as DISTAR and mastery learning—train principals just as they do teachers in order to insure that they carry out their critical responsibilities of monitoring and evaluating instruction.

As for the issue of leadership, it may be true that leaders are born and not made. But a wide range of observers believe that providing opportunities for would-be principals to intern under some of their more experienced, successful peers would go a long way toward instilling the desired qualities. "Universities can provide an academic and philosophical background, but that doesn't mean that principals are prepared for specific situations," said Leonard Gregory, chairman of the department of education administration at Indiana University. "The solution is to let him face problems in a controlled situation. It is possible to teach old dogs new tricks, if you're willing to work with them, show them the way."

Autonomy

In order for principals to improve their students' achievement, they have to have the authority to determine who teaches at their school (presuming they know what qualities to look for) and what instructional methods are used (presuming they're equipped to make this decision). Without these powers, principals are provided with a wealth of excuses for not holding themselves or their staffs accountable for student achievement; it will always be someone else's fault.

However, greater autonomy in itself does not guarantee accountability. Instead of greater flexibility to solve problems, it can set the stage for a laissez-faire climate in which principals are satisfied with low student achievement or blame the students themselves. For example, the San Diego School System gives its principals a great amount of responsibility and authority; a Rand Corporation report described the relationship between the central administration and its schools as "loosely coupled." But a court-appointed team, studying 23 racially isolated, low-achieving San Diego schools, found in 1980 that the following complacent response of a principal of a school (where sixth graders were reading at the 28th percentile) was typical of the attitude of the district's principals: "We feel that _____ School is providing the opportunity for quality education for all students. We perceive no major problems."

Evaluation

There is only one way to evaluate principals. As the court-appointed team in San Diego suggested: "Principals . . . should be continuously evaluated in terms of their students' achievements. Retention in leadership positions at all levels should be contingent on the attainment of established goals. The leadership cannot accept failure, and . . . dedication and commitment has to flow from the top down."

No immediate action was taken on this recommendation in San Diego. And, according to the elementary school principals' association, no major school system has taken this step. In the few places where strict accountability measures have been proposed for principals, their professional organizations have said they would accept them if they were allowed long-term contracts in exchange, a trade-off which would defeat the purpose of more rigorous evaluations. As Nat Hentoff put it in his *Village Voice* article: "There should be no tenure for principals. Students who leave [their] school[s] get no tenure in the real world."

To summarize, then, the way to spawn more effective principals, more "Carol Russos" in a school system is to pick principals who understand instruction and are willing to meet student performance goals, evaluate them annually according to how well their students are achieving, and make their jobs contingent on satisfactory progress. Probably no single change in present practices would go further toward improving America's public schools than this.

5

Case White A Revisited: *Edison School*

I n 1975, researchers from Michigan State University spent a month observing the workings of the Edison School. As sociologists, they viewed schools as small, distinct worlds, each characterized by its own "school climate" or unique set of staff and student attitudes, expectations, and perceptions. Their theory was that the quality of this school climate—the nature of each school's particular social system—had a strong, independent effect on student achievement.

Edison is one of five elementaries in the 3700-pupil Madison School District, which serves the southern half of Madison Heights, Michigan, a virtually all-white, blue-collar community a few miles north of Detroit. The school has about 400 students in grades kindergarten through six; it's fairly run-down and sits in a neighborhood of small homes bordering the Chrysler Expressway. The researchers chose to visit Edison because it appeared to be a maverick school: Although many of its students came from low-income families (including a substantial number of first- and second-generation migrants from Appalachia), they registered relatively high marks on the 1974 statewide assessment test. And once they spent some time at the school, the researchers' initial suspicions based on the students' test scores were confirmed. They reported finding a decidedly positive school climate, one that seemed to account for Edison's outstanding achievement record and one with many attributes worth emulating.

According to their case study of Edison, which they labeled "White A," the school's principal primarily was concerned with student achievement; his staff viewed him as an instructional leader, rather than simply as an administrator. His goal was to visit each teacher's classroom at least 30 times during the school year. "Almost without exception teachers in this school, through their behavior and comments, indicated that they respected their principal," the study said.

All of Edison's students were in a primary-grade basic skills program, designed to insure a minimum level of mastery in reading. Almost all classroom time was devoted to academic instruction; teachers worked students hard. Students needing extra help were not stigmatized by being pulled out of their regular classes for remedial programs; specially funded aides worked with whole classes rather than just certain children. There was little separation of children into ability groups. And interested parents were enlisted in the service of the school's clear instructional goals. For instance, about 30 parents formed a "bucket brigade" in which they came to Edison and worked with individual children, using prepared buckets of materials to teach specific skills.

The school's staff had high expectations of its students. Few pupils were written off as uneducable; all were expected to be at normal levels for their grades in the basics. To this end, teachers used positive reinforcement in an appropriate way to motivate students. They often divided up their classes into teams for academic games, fostering cooperation and interest in learning. In the school's hallways, they carefully monitored student behavior, leading pupils in quiet lines every time movement was necessary.

So, based on these observations, the Michigan State researchers concluded that Edison was a special kind of low-income school, one where the staff was "committed to providing its students with an education on par with that normally reserved for middle-class youngsters." Wilbur Brookover, the sociologist who headed the research project, later recalled: "Edison isn't the best school in Michigan, but it was a darn good one. It wasn't perfect, but it demonstrated that all kids can learn—even poor, white ones."

Four years later, however, the observer who spent some time in Edison's classrooms and talking with its staff, students, and parents might have wondered if he had stumbled into the wrong school. By the fall of 1979, something had happened to this elementary school. Edison still had the same principal; its teacher turnover had been low; its students came from the same kinds of background. But almost every one of the positive attributes identified by the university researchers was no longer to be found.

Gone were the basic skills program and the top-down emphasis on academics. The school's principal of nine years, John Hood, said he had grown "disillusioned" with that program's "narrow focus" and dropped it in favor of a "more humanistic approach concentrating on students' feelings and the quality of day-to-day life in the school." He described Edison's previous system as "mechanistic" by contrast. "We were teaching all these little skills, but there was no synthesis," Hood said. "The kids could only go so far. The affective domain is much more important than the cognitive, anyway."

So in the school's main hallway, a banner boasted: "Edison is a good place to be. Someone cares about you and me." Edison's teachers were concentrating more on music and art then ever before. Kindergarteners were spending some of their school days sitting in a circle talking about their behavior. And Hood was particularly proud of a program in which he showed students pictures of themselves to prompt discussions of their self-images. "The kids are better off now," he said. "They're not nearly so beaten down, as unhappy, as oppressed."

In the same vein, Edison no longer had schoolwide academic objectives. The school's staff even had trouble finding recent test score averages. And Hood said he never discusses the test scores with teachers—let alone holds them accountable for student improvement. He added he evaluates teachers according to individual goals they've set for themselves, ones that often involve exclusively personal matters—rather than student progress. "I'm trying to reduce the impersonal quality of the workplace," he said. "If a teacher can talk with me about her husband's drinking problem, then her efficiency will improve because she'll feel better about herself."

But few teachers said Hood had talked with them about these evaluations; the idea of revealing their personal problems to him sent some into gales of laughter. That Hood might serve as the school's instructional leader provoked a similar reaction. "That's a farce," said one teacher. And it was basically the same with Hood's stress on the "quality of day-to-day life" at Edison. "You know that motto in the hall about, 'Edison is a good place to be,' " said another teacher. "None of the kids can read it, and no one here really gives a shit."

Hood was not without his supporters on the staff. "He believes in children," said one teacher. "They weren't able to really learn with the old basic skills approach. His new philosophy is rubbing off on us." But many others viewed him as "mercurial" and "vacillating." Most had given up on looking to him for support; a few were outright fearful of him. "Ideas come and go here," said one longtime teacher.

"Hood is constantly trying new things. One minute, it's brute force; another minute, it's something else."

For his part, Hood allowed he didn't get into Edison's classrooms very often, because he spent most of his time in his office "dealing with day-to-day administration, waiting for crises to occur, up to my knees in alligators. I'd like to see myself as an instructional leader, but in reality I'm just reacting to crises." Hood disagreed, though, with teachers' assessment of his style of leadership. "Mercurial? I'd prefer 'nimble,' " he said. "You know, they desperately want me to tell them what to do, to wield a whip over them. And I won't do that."

At Edison, then, teachers were doing essentially what they wanted to do in classes. Often that meant wasted time, unfocused lessons, unenergetic instruction, inattentive students, and behavior problems. "No one is taking responsibility for education here," complained a teacher who's been at the school for four years. "No one pays any attention to the product. No one is monitoring teaching. There are no goals. People aren't pulling together, or excited about what's happening here. It's unreal, amazing. No one goes into the classrooms."

The only recognizable vestige of the Michigan State study was that Edison's teachers still liked to conduct team games with their students; they seemed to turn to this activity, however, when all else had failed to bring order and interest to their classes. The school's remedial program had been changed so that individual pupils were pulled out of class to work with specially funded aides. "One child told me he didn't care what I did with him—as long as I didn't call him 'dumb,' " said an aide. "I asked him why, and he said, 'Kids who leave for extra help are dumb. . . . Aren't they?' " The parents' "bucket brigade" was gone; the creator of the program, Barb Thompson, explained the "staff dropped it believing that parents weren't interested any more, but what may have happened is that the parents were so turned off by the principal they didn't want to come to school."

Also absent were many of the quiet, orderly scenes in the school's halls. Children came back from recess on the run, pushing and shoving. One child three days in a row yelled, "Niggerskins, niggerskins," at another who was foreign-born. A teacher yanked another student's arm. "Jerk! Jerk!" she cried, shaking him. "You're acting like a jerk!" And as for the staff's strong sense of high expectations, that, too, seemed to have dissolved. In one upper-grade class, students were frequently called "retardos" and "animals." Said a kindergarten teacher, "You can tell real early that some kids aren't going to make it. . . . I don't see any of the kids in this class going on to college."

Added a longtime third-grade teacher: "Perhaps I should have high expectations. . . . Shouldn't I? But some of these children come from very low backgrounds. Their families are transient, here one night and gone the next, running from the bill collector. With 32 of them, you can't possibly spend all your time with some while the others get nothing. Whatever you try, there're smart ones and slower ones. Some will graduate from high school, but a lot won't," she said, going back to her grade book to check on exactly which ones will make it. "One . . . two . . . three . . . maybe five." She lowered her voice. "Well, you saw that one over there. That type of child is always behind—very low I.Q. You can't do much with that kind."

In 1979, then, Edison's school climate was far more acrimonious than positive, far more unfocused than reflective of a schoolwide commitment to high achievement, and unfortunately far more typical than exceptional. All of this— the absence of instructional leadership, of an academic thrust, of high expectations—was disconcerting enough on its own, without even attempting to relate it to the state of affairs so glowingly described by the Michigan State researchers some four years earlier. It was, though, only the tip of the trouble at this elementary school.

* * *

They sit on plaid furniture amid a wealth of middle-American bric-a-brac in the small living room of Shirley Hughes's tidy, two-story house of 15 years. The four housewives are essentially what is left of the Edison School's once active PTA. Like so many others in Madison Heights, their husbands work in jobs linked to the failing auto industry. They talk a bit of the hidden poverty here—the many retired and disabled, the young couples who can't hold jobs, the increasing number of single parents. But their conversation quickly turns to what is happening at their children's school. They are worried for themselves and others. They don't understand why they have been shut out of their school. And they are starved to know what they can do.

"I'd like to know what's going on," says Mrs. Hughes, Edison's PTA president. "I'd like to be informed for once. . . . My daughter's in the fifth grade; it's hard for her to write a sentence." Another woman chimes in: "Mine's in the sixth grade and can't multiply or divide so well." Another quickly adds: "Mine can't either. They're doing nothing for him."

"The kids are running the teachers," says Linda Selimi, the PTA's treasurer. "They're playing too many games, instead of learning." Mrs. Hughes joins back in: "There's no order in the school. Kids are running all over, throwing toilet paper. Each little kid has to fight to get into the door." And Jana Bacheldor, a PTA vice president, says: "Kids used to have to sit on the floor to eat their lunches. Other schools are for kids; this one is not. They don't give a damn at that school."

They all want more homework. They all want someone to

take charge of the discipline problem. And none of them says she's had any success in communicating with Hood. "He accuses us of wanting him to use Gestapo tactics," explains Mrs. Hughes. They don't know what happened to the "bucket brigade." They don't know why the school's emphasis on the basic skills suddenly was dropped. They raised $800 so that fathers in the community could build some new playground equipment; they say Hood told them they couldn't do it. "He just sits in his office, and that's it," says Mrs. Bacheldor. "He wants us to fall on our faces." Adds Mrs. Hughes: "You can't let him intimidate you. He just talks you in circles."

Hood owns to being "cynical about the role of parents. I haven't had a goal to involve parents. I've just let things die naturally as opposed to trying to sustain community involvement. I see the importance of it, but you can get a roomful of them [parents] dickering among themselves, and it just sabotages anything you're trying to do. My first agenda is to keep them from interfering with the process of education."

There is a deep breach here between Edison and its community, one that apparently remains unresolved even though it became obvious several years previous when a petition was taken to the local school board asking that Hood be removed from his job. "The petition was just the tip of the iceberg," says a teacher. "There were gangs of kids running around the building. There was a lot of paranoia spreading among the staff." Madison school board member Elva Mills says the board dealt with the petition by "suggesting that he [Hood] try to be more conscientious." All Hood will say about it is, "I've got my political enemies out there." In his defense, another Edison parent, Linda Golembeck, just writes the whole affair off to the work of "troublemakers who wanted to run the school in their own way."

In the meantime, however, the controversy all but wiped out Edison's PTA, which held a meeting in the 1978–79 school year with only five parents in attendance. "We've tried to find out what happened to that petition," says Mrs. Andrews. "The board said it didn't have to tell us."

"What gives him so much power?" asks Mrs. Bacheldor. "That's what I'd like to know. I'd put my kids in a private school, if I could afford it. I don't know what we're going to do, but I'm not going to sit around. I'm going to fight with all my might."

* * *

Wilbur Brookover, a professor of sociology, education, and urban and metropolitan affairs at Michigan State University in East Lansing, Michigan, has been studying school achievement since 1939. He was an expert witness for the plaintiffs at the *Brown v. Topeka Board of Education* trial, the lead case resulting in the landmark school desegregation decision by the U.S. Supreme Court in 1954. His concept of school climate is based on a social-psychological theory of learning, which holds that people learn and do the things that others around them expect them to do.

Brookover's main research interest has been in establishing a relationship between low staff expectations and a high sense of futility on the part of students, and in examining the effect of these feelings on student achievement. In this type of research, teachers are asked questions like, "What percentage of the students in your class do you expect to complete high school?" Students are asked questions to determine if they believe, "People like me will never do well in school even though they try hard." Brookover said he moved on to the broader question of, "What's different about schools with similar student bodies and distinctly different levels of achievement?," to counteract widely publicized research by James Coleman and Christopher Jencks. Coleman's work has been taken to mean that students' family backgrounds determine how well they will do in school; and Jenck's work has been interpreted to imply that schools have no independent effect on who gets ahead in society. Brookover did not accept either idea.

"Case White A," Brookover's study of the Edison School, was one of four similar case studies, comparing two pairs of black and white, high-achieving and low-achieving elementaries. It has been included in a more extensive, more statistically oriented work, published in 1979 as *School Social Systems and Student Achievement.* The sub-title of that book is *Schools Can Make A Difference,* and its primary conclusion is that the climate of staff and student attitudes, expectations, and perceptions at each school explain student achievement patterns just as much as do pupils' family backgrounds. Put simply, the book describes a kind of self-fulfilling prophecy in which high staff expectations and resulting actions lead to students' feeling that they can master their work; this sense of confidence, in turn, leads to high achievement by students. In low-achieving schools, the book says, staffs tend to perceive students' abilities to be low and act accordingly, and so students feel that the school is stacked against them and end up achieving little.

Along the same lines, Brookover and his associate, Lawrence Lezotte, have examined six improving and two declining elementaries to determine changes in their characteristics coincident with changes in student achievement. Among the findings of that 1977 study are:

• Improving school staffs tend to believe all their students can master the basics and are more likely to hold increasingly higher levels of expectations of their students. Declining school staffs tend to believe that students' abilities are too low for them to master the basics and they are less likely to believe their students will complete high school or college.

• Improving school teachers and principals are more likely to assume responsibility for teaching the basics and to spend more time on direct instruction in reading. Declining school staffs are more likely to place the responsibility for learning on parents or students and to spend less time on direct reading instruction.

• Improving school principals are more likely to be instructional leaders and strong disciplinarians and to take responsibility for evaluating student achievement. Declining school principals tend to be more permissive and more interested in public relations and informal relationships with their staffs.

• Improving school staffs show a greater acceptance of the concept of accountability in the form of using student test scores to evaluate their efforts. Those at declining schools tend to reject the relevance of assessment data.

One uncertain finding of this study involved differences in the level of parent involvement between improving and declining schools. Less overall parent involvement was found in the improving schools, but higher levels of *parent initiated* contacts were noted. "We started from the premise that poor people often give schools too much credit and not enough examination," said Brookover. "If anything, the people don't know what to do and often aren't part of the answer. The declining schools often were good at public relations. They had parents coming and going, totally cooled out. You have to be careful of the role of parents."

* * *

It's ten minutes of nine on a Friday morning in a sixth-grade classroom on the second floor of the Edison School, and the students are reluctantly filtering in. They talk and move about the room as their teacher takes lunch money and attendance. There is no work on their desks. "I can tell it's Friday," the teacher says loudly. "You know it and I know it. Now let's stop it." The students quiet momentarily and then resume talking.

Two minutes later, she angrily flicks the lights off and on. "What is this?" she yells. "What is going on today?" And then she goes back to her administrative chores. The students continue talking.

After ten minutes, she tells them to take out their math from yesterday. "Until you quiet down," she says, "we won't do our science experiment." The students ignore her. "OK," she yells again, "since we're not settling down, let's get out our social studies."

Now the students finally get down to work. But they have both their math and social studies before them. And so a procession of children comes to the front of the room one by one to ask the teacher what they're supposed to be doing. Within five minutes, a third of the students are out of their seats—at the pencil sharpener or in the bathroom. "Either work quietly or do something together," she tells them, starting to set up the science experiment.

"This is a bad day because we're doing an experiment," she whispers to a visitor. Asked why she is doing it, she answers: "Because it's in the science book . . . ," her voice trailing off as she hears herself.

"Now look, enough is enough," she says loudly, as she tries to run an electric cord for the experiment across a row of students. "The rest of you be quiet or I'll give you something else to do."

It's 9:30 a.m. The students have had it, and so has the teacher. In desperation, she tells them to put down their work to play a game. They divide into four teams to compete in doing math problems. An hour later, they are still working on their fourth problem, and she is talking with one student. Most of the class is sitting, looking bored. Twenty minutes later, still nothing is happening. Finally at 11 o'clock, she tells them to take out a piece of paper for a "creative writing" assignment.

She warns the students that she's more interested in their ideas on today's topic—"something on wheels"—than whether their "paragraphs and commas are in the right place." She further instructs: "The typical sixth-grade story about something on wheels is about a car rescued from a car lot that gets driven around and wrecked and ends up in a junkyard." After 15 minutes, she is still telling the students what not to write about.

One child gets excited and offers an idea. "If you have such good ideas," she snaps back, "I'd wish you'd keep them to yourself."

"I've done this for so many years," she tells the whole class, ending her discourse, "I tend to think you understand. Do you? Do you understand this?"

In two and a half hours this morning, the students have been working perhaps an average of half an hour. Some haven't done a single thing; all are ready for lunch. And the teacher is just about at her wit's end. What is happening here—the wasted time, the failure to instruct, the so-called "discipline problems" as a direct consequence of having nothing to do—is somewhat typical of the Edison School. "We're professionals," one teacher says. "We know what we're doing." But signs to the contrary are all around: large numbers of students always lined up at the pencil sharpeners; students constantly leaving classes to go to the bathroom or just getting up and walking out for no apparent reason; teachers referring to Thursdays and Fridays—days when they have to teach all day because there are no special classes—as "bloody days"; fifth graders who never get homework; and teachers conducting question-and-answer drills by talking to one side of the class, ignoring any child who doesn't know an answer.

There are exceptions: classes where order and instruction reign. But as one teacher puts it: "The norm here is mediocrity." Even Hood admits, "Yes, the staff and students could stand a push. I don't know why I haven't done it. It's not something to ignore." It is not so much bad teaching as *nonteaching.* And unfortunately, Edison is not an isolated example; classes like these abound in America's public schools.

"Why kids learn anything here is a mystery to me," says an Edison teacher. "Their parents are very much into just surviving. They don't give the kids what they need. And then they turn to us and still don't get it." Indeed, by Brookover's measures, Edison appears to have become a declining school rather than an improving school. And the school's record on the Michigan State Assessment Test backs that up. From 1978 to 1979, the percentage of students mastering three-quarters of the reading objectives fell from 70 to 60 percent, and the percentage mastering less than a quarter of the same objectives rose from 6 to 17 percent. But Brookover's equation for school effectiveness cannot be applied so neatly. For even though Edison's achievement is falling, it is still higher (in reading) than when Brookover's researchers chose to visit the school.

Edison offers two lessons. The first is the vast gulf between research in the social sciences and the realities of complex institutions like elementary schools. The school's history illustrates "there is no such thing as a single characteristic which accounts for schools being exemplary or not," says Gilbert Austin, a University of Maryland researcher. Brookover agrees: "There's great danger in looking at single factors."

The second and perhaps more important message is that schools do not exist in a vacuum. They are vulnerable to an incredible array of internal and external influences. If they are exemplary, it's because of a rather delicate set of balances which can easily be destroyed. Says Tom Tomlinson, a National Institute of Education program officer long intrigued by the problem of understanding schools: "They're like dinosaurs—great beasts with delicate constitutions who tend to suffer dramatically with slight shifts in their atmosphere." Or as Hood himself says, "Change is the mode here. It's possible to make any kind of changes in a school."

* * *

Change also marked the field of educational research in the 1960s and 1970s, particularly in response to the critical question, What makes schools work well for all children? During that time, the prevailing method of inquiry shifted from a quantitative, input-output model to one which views schools in a more qualitative, organic light. Correspondingly, researchers' interests are no longer focused on what is true for all schools so much as on what accounts for the successes of certain exceptional schools. And as a result, social science has been alternately confident and then pessimistic about the prospects for school reform—with commensurate political effects.

In the early 1960s, educators were generally confident that all children could be taught, given adequate resources. It was believed that differences in achievement among schools reflected varying resources. The Elementary and Secondary School Act of 1965, which funded the Title I program, the first major federal compensatory education effort, was grounded in the conventional wisdom that bridging the achievement gap was a simple matter of equalizing resources.

However, this view quickly was shattered by sociologist James Coleman's 743-page report, *Equality of Educational Opportunity*, the most extensive survey of the nation's educational system ever conducted. The Coleman report, released July 3, 1966, had been requested by the Justice Department so it could document educational discrimination. But one of its main conclusions, based on the achievement patterns of some 600,000 students in thousands of schools in every region in the country, was that educational resources were more equally shared than had been thought. It was found that the family backgrounds of pupils is the factor most related to achievement and that variations in school facilities, curriculum, and staffs have little independent effect. Coleman was widely misinterpreted as saying that schools don't make any difference in children's lives; however, his actual point—that school-related factors don't account for differences in students' achievement—was strong enough by itself. His findings were challenged in some quarters as the product of imprecise analysis and improper statistical techniques, but several later analyses of his raw data came to the same overriding conclusions. And the results of the early Title I evaluations gave Coleman further credence: While the federal program was successful in equalizing resources, it failed to produce consistent improvements in student achievement.

This new pessimism about the possibilities for reforming schools neatly dovetailed with the political climate set by the Nixon administration, which was antagonistic to many of the "War on Poverty" programs. It was to be fueled by Arthur Jensen's 1969 study, in which he argued that schools cannot bring black students' achievement up to the same level as that of whites because of inherited genetic differences; and by Christopher Jencks' 1972 study, in which he found that luck plays a more important role than both family background and the quality of schooling in determining students' future incomes. "We are not suggesting that nothing makes a difference, or that nothing works," declared a 1971 Rand Corporation review of the current research on school effectiveness. "Rather we are saying that research has found nothing that consistently and unambiguously makes a difference in students' outcomes."

But George Weber, then associate director of the Council for Basic Education, believed this research was simply "sophisticated nonsense" that confused "correlation with causation" and "extended a general situation to a universal truth." And in 1970, Weber began a nationwide search for successful inner-city schools with which to challenge the rising acceptance of the idea that nothing could be done about low achievement, particularly among low-income students. In a report released in late 1971, *Inner-City Children Can Be Taught To Read*, Weber described four schools in which achievement levels were at or above national norms—two in Manhattan, one in Kansas City, Missouri, and one in Los Angeles.

Weber's technique of finding exceptionally successful low-income schools (mavericks) and then comparing them to less-successful schools with comparable student bodies was soon emulated by many researchers across the country, including Brookover and Lezotte in Michigan. Although their studies yielded slightly different sets of factors for success, a common formula emerged by the end of the 1970s. As outlined by Ron Edmonds, a Harvard University researcher and senior assistant to the chancellor of the New York City Schools, the identified characteristics of effective schools include:

• Strong instructional leadership marshalling the school's resources toward common purposes.

• A climate of high expectations in which no children are allowed to fall below minimum standards of achievement.

• An orderly, but not rigid, school atmosphere conducive to instruction.

• A clear, shared emphasis on the basic skills which takes precedence over all other school activities.

• Frequent, careful monitoring of pupil progress.

With these studies, confidence in the possibilities of reforming schools, so that all children could be served, bloomed again among many researchers—so much so that they were anything but shy about attempting to apply their findings to actual schools. In their view, schools could no longer be seen as simple "black boxes," into which resources are poured and out of which student achievement flowed. Instead, they saw schools as living organisms, which could be changed willfully. By the 1979–80 school year, projects intended to change schools using the characteristics of already effective schools were underway in three cities: in 20 racially isolated Milwaukee schools as part of an out-of-court settlement of a desegregation suit; in seven Pontiac, Michigan, schools under a school district contract with Brookover and Lezotte; and in about ten New York City elementaries under Edmonds's "School Improvement Project."

Edmonds's project was perhaps the most ambitious. To each of the ten schools, he has assigned an outside, experienced "liaison," who began working with staff members to emulate the characteristics of effective schools, including strong instructional leadership, high expectations, and better use of tests. The project is a long-term effort to change the organizational dynamics of the selected schools; in the beginning, care was taken not to threaten their staffs with too much change too soon. Said Gwen Thomas, a liaison to an elementary in the Bronx, "You can't jump on teachers' backs. That's not the way to do it. If you're going to attack attitudinal problems, you have to use good human relations."

Edmonds, both a researcher and a practitioner, views himself as "not a distant, impartial social observer, but a passionate party to the enterprise." And he believes that much of the problem in attempting to reform schools is a matter of belief and politics, rather than educational technology or social science. "Repudiation of the social science notion that family background is the principal cause of pupil acquisition of basic school skills is probably prerequisite to successful reform of public schooling for the children of the poor," he wrote. "We can whenever, and wherever we choose, successfully teach all children whose schooling is of interest to us. We already know more than we need, in order to do this. Whether we do it must finally depend on how we feel about the fact we haven't so far. . . . The great problem in schooling is that we know how to teach in ways that keep some children from learning almost anything and we often proceed thus in dealing with the children of the poor."

He believes, then, that pupil performance "derives not from family background, but from schools' response to family background. This school system [New York's]—just like every other in the country—has been badly serving the lower one-third of the city. It's not conspiratorial, or nefarious; it's just part of a national norm. Left to their own devices, social service agencies—schools included—serve only those they think they must. And when they don't think they need to provide service, they don't. There's nothing extraordinary about this. Why is it if you pay garbage men to work eight hours a day, they only pick up trash on certain streets and not on others? They're just following the nature of public servants in delivering public services."

So Edmonds's project is an attempt to provide the selected schools with not only some additional resources and expertise, but also a political impetus for their staffs to perform better—a pressure that is otherwise lacking in most low-income schools. In essence, whether they readily accept it or not, the staffs of the schools in his project have been handed a charge to not settle for anything less than the results they would expect if they were teaching at middle-class schools. "What happens at middle-class schools when their reading and math scores fall off?" Edmonds asked. "The parents raise hell, and then educators do something differently. Why would they bother to change, unless someone is making them? It happens at some low-income schools, too; it's just not done enough there."

While Edmonds's project may prove to be successful, it has come under fire from other researchers primarily because his list of effective school characteristics is little more than a general, descriptive outline, a "laundry list." Said Tom Tomlinson, of the National Institute of Education,

"The problem with Edmonds's theories is that they're conspiratorial and self-evident, and they don't tell us anything about how to specifically create better schools. How do you define things like effective leadership or school climate? It gets very tricky, very soft, when you're trying to explain the connections to student achievement. It is, indeed, a fragile equation."

Edmonds acknowledged these criticisms but stressed they should not dim confidence in his approach to changing schools. "No one thing explains school climate," he said, "just as no one thing explains the origins of institutional behavior. But with both institutions and individuals, we're able to change behavior without being able to explain how we do it. It's just like we know that reward works better than punishment in changing individuals' behavior. We don't know why it works. And we don't have to know why. We just do it because it works."

Looking At Your School: School Climate

The concept of school climate represents the latest development in the research on what makes for effective schools. It is the product of looking at the webs of human interaction within schools, rather than isolated factors. And so, while it may provide a more accurate basis for describing the internal dynamics of schools, it does not necessarily lead to a specific prescription for improving schools. It is an intangible ethos, rather than a concrete program. It is hard to identify and measure and even more difficult to alter. Attempting to change the climate of a school means having to deal directly with the standards of appropriate behavior and beliefs set by adults in the school. And it usually will mean having to break down the considerable walls of institutional inertia.

"One of the problems in eduction is that we don't have a good model for changing organizations," said Lezotte of Michigan State. "Unlike Ford, which closes down its plants to retool before each new year's models, we try to change schools on the dead-run. It's much harder."

In their school climate improvement project in the Pontiac school system, Lezotte and Brookover have borrowed heavily from the self-help model employed by groups like Weight Watchers, a model that focuses not so much on individuals as on developing group support for individual change. They believe that changing an individual's behavior will not be successful unless the norms or standards, set by those in the group around him also are altered. In Weight Watchers, each member checks in with the group regularly, is weighed, and receives positive or negative reactions from the other group members on how he is progressing in losing weight. Members, thus, are forced by peer pressure to confront their own actions and attitudes regularly (in this case, towards food and eating). Likewise in schools, Brookover and Lezotte suggest that this model can serve as the basis for both individual checkups and regular staff meetings in which members report and are checked on what they've been doing to:

• Reduce students' feelings of futility.

• Increase their evaluation of students' ability to learn.

• Communicate a higher level of expectations to all students.

• Clearly define common goals for their students.

• Demonstrate their commitment to all students reading at their proper grade levels.

• Give clear, unambiguous, and positive reinforcement to students when appropriate.

As with the Weight Watchers' meetings, the two researchers say, the success of these checkups in altering school climate (and improving schools) is dependent on the level of approval and recognition the group as a whole awards certain behaviors and attitudes—in this case, those that lead to high student achievement. A necessary precondition for this kind of support group—in schools and elsewhere—is that members must share the belief that collective and individual change is possible, if they want to attempt it. The next step suggested by the researchers is a "realistic appraisal" of both the current behaviors and beliefs at the school and of the high degree of commitment required to make substantial improvements. It is not necessary at the outset, though, for school staffs to swallow the much more threatening tenet that all children can learn. "We don't try to change anyone's beliefs by talking to them," said Lezotte. "I don't believe that can be done. We tell them to believe what they will—about poor kids, about minorities—for the time being, but just behave as if they can do the job. We say, 'Give us the benefit of the doubt. Try it, and see what happens.'

"What usually happens is they start to see different outcomes among their students than they expected. And so they then change their attitudes. The only way to change the climate of beliefs at a school is to first work on behavior."

To this end, their "School Climate Activities Training Program" for the Pontiac schools goes into great detail on the principles of mastery learning, the importance of principals being instructional leaders, increasing "time on task" in classes, and the productive use of group learning games. However, Lezotte noted, "If teachers feel that achievement is not their responsibility and is the fault of parents, then they'll assume that very little can be done about it, and won't even try. It's the kind of ethic that violates the contract between schools and society. Teachers ultimately have to come to understand that if they pick up their paychecks week after week, then they have a social responsibility to teach all children."

6

The Limits of Human Relations: *Byck School*

The heavyset black woman perched nervously on the edge of one of the cushioned chairs in the principal's office, constantly gesturing as she talked about her foster daughter's problems. Tears came to her tired eyes as she told how the little girl had been beaten by her parents and how the child would sneak over to her house when she hadn't been fed. The woman started to shake a little; she was under pressure. She was doing everything in her power to provide a better home for the child, but still there were times when the girl "wasn't quite right," when she stood "in front of the mirror and talked to herself." And now there were problems in school, which is why the woman had walked from her nearby home on Louisville's west side to see Matt Benningfield and Janice Walker. She knew they would help.

Sitting next to the woman, Benningfield, the Byck School's principal, took her hand and appeared to listen intently, nodding reassurance every so often. When she had finished telling her story, he turned to Mrs. Walker, the school's instructional coordinator, and asked her to change seats with him and go over the child's records with the woman. The three then talked at length about the little girl's lagging performance in her classes and about the emotional scars that apparently still remained from her previous home. Benningfield and Mrs. Walker took turns encouraging the woman to keep on working with the child, to keep on trying. And they offered to place her foster daughter in a special class for a while so she could receive more attention, which the woman agreed might be best. At the end of the 45-minute conference, the woman smiled a bit; she appeared relieved. As she left, she reached up to give both Benningfield and Mrs. Walker long, tight hugs, and everyone's eyes swelled with a few more tears.

It was early in the morning, the start of another varied day at Byck, Louisville's most highly regarded inner-city school—a school with a remarkable history of meeting its communities' needs through careful attention to the art of human relations. After this, their first conference of the day, the school's two administrators seemed somewhat drawn. But more parents would be coming to Byck to sit in classes or talk about their children's education. And each—rich or poor, black or white—would be met with the same concern, the same friendly, tender touch. Each would become part of Byck's growing family.

Parents would come to a first-grade room to talk with the teacher about preparations for a cookout to be held before an upcoming soccer match between Byck's teachers and its fifth graders. An elderly woman, all dressed up, would walk in off the street unexpectedly to ask if she could help out. Benningfield smiled at her and sent her to the school's Head Start class with little fanfare. "I guess she just wants to be with kids," he said a bit sheepishly, as she went down the hallway unescorted.

The school's secretary, security guard, maintenance man, and lunchroom manager would come to Benningfield's office for one of their weekly planning sessions during which they would talk about everything from a shortage of toilet paper to some recent improvements in student behavior. "I don't know what we're doing right," the security guard said, mentioning two students by name. "But they're really coming around. It's great to see." Later, teachers would forego their lounge at lunchtime to eat at the tables in Mrs. Walker's office and talk about the progress of particular children. A teacher's problems with a math text sent Mrs. Walker to her long shelf of books to find more appropriate materials. "Teachers get here and they don't want to leave," said a music teacher in between bites of her sandwich.

A reporter from one of Louisville's newspapers would stop by to work on her monthly series about a first-grade class at the school. Benningfield didn't know she was in the building and wasn't really concerned about it. "You've got to have a certain trust level," he said. "We say come in, but we can't guarantee what you'll find." A University of Louisville professor, Byck's new PTA president, also would drop in so that Benningfield could explain the possible effects of a districtwide reorganization plan. "Matt doesn't pretend to have all the answers," the professor said. "There's an openness to change here. It's brought all kinds of different people together."

Another white parent, herself a teacher, would drive some 15 miles across town from the middle-class suburbs in the east end of Jefferson County to talk about her second grader with Mrs. Walker. "He's doing a job on us," the mother said. "He's not doing as much as he could; he likes to dawdle. He should be making As, instead of Bs." Mrs. Walker agreed with the woman, and the two talked with the child about the need for more work on his writing. "You can do better," the mother told the little boy. He nodded. "Do we get to see some improvement the first thing in the morning?" Mrs. Walker asked. And he nodded again.

"I heard the staff here makes an extra effort," the woman said to another visitor as she left Byck. "They listen to you; Byck is unique. It's an awful long drive from where we live, but it's more of our home school than the one in my neighborhood."

All around Jefferson County and most particularly in the four disparate communities that send their childen to the elementary school, such sentiments are commonplace. Everyone loves Byck. And invariably, they can't say enough in favor of Matt Benningfield, a principal who has parlayed a "little bit of the Good Book" and some modern philosophies into a decided knack for making his incredibly diverse students, staff, and parents feel good about being part of his school. More than anything, Byck's growing reputation as a successful school is testimony to Benningfield's ability to sell his oft-stated belief that communication and sharing both decisions and responsibilities make for a better school.

Benningfield, 47, came to Louisville from the small country town of Stanton, near Kentucky's Red River Gorge. He still owns a grocery store there, which he tends on weekends. Byck's principal for 17 years, he headed a federally funded night school during the turbulent 1960s. It provided his introduction to the ins and outs of working with inner-city communities, an art at which he apparently has become a virtuoso. He wears aviator glasses and three-piece, pinstriped suits, has a soft, slightly southern accent, and likes to sit in his office and talk about "personal growth," about "internalizing responsibilities," about "sharing pools of knowledge." In the 1960s, he was trained in the ways of "sensitivity" groups; in the early 1970s, he learned about the principles of behavior modification. His "Byckian philosophy" reflects both. "What I'm really talking about," he says, "is a marriage of both [behaviorist B. F.] Skinner and [humanist Carl] Rogers. You use positive reinforcement to straighten out the school; and then once all the students are in line, you let some of Carl's good feelings come in. It's a family relationship." If Benningfield is a salesman and human relations is his product, he is setting some local records according to his customers.

"Byck is participatory democracy institutionalized, an educational democracy," said one of the dozen or so white, middle-class parents who opted to leave their children at the school after first sending them there reluctantly under Jefferson County's court-ordered desegregation plan. "Byck flies in the face of everywhere else in the school district. It's not failure oriented. The principal gives power over to others. He treats teachers like adults. There's a kind of accountability you get from parents always being in the school. You can't measure it in test scores. It's not quantifiable. You either believe in it or you don't."

And in this county, where court-ordered desegregation was met with great resistance and at times violence, the story of Byck would appear to be a textbook example of how to make busing work well, of how to flexibly respond to events that can tear apart a school.

* * *

Before the predominantly black Louisville school system merged with the larger, mostly white Jefferson County schools and busing between the two became a fact of life, Byck was a vastly different place. Almost all Byck students were black and poor then, and all but three of its classrooms received federal aid. For the first five years of the 1970s, the school had a highly structured curriculum in its primary grades, the University of Kansas's "behavior analysis" program, which relies heavily on rewarding student achievement with tokens that can be spent on recreational activities. Test scores from this time show that Byck's students were progressing at their grade levels, outdoing those in Louisville's other inner-city schools. So back then as later,

Byck was known as a good school by the black parents living in the small, brick and wood shotgun homes in its immediate neighborhood, the Russell area.

When rioting tore at the community in the late 1960s, for instance, local residents wrote the words "Soul Brother" across Byck's front door to protect the building. "It never was an ordinary school," said Maude Carbin, head of Russell's improvement association. "And Matt Benningfield was no ordinary principal. Byck had everything a child would want. You could go all over Russell, and people wouldn't have anything to say against Matt Benningfield; he's a beautiful man. He could run for mayor of Russell."

The trouble is, the 1975 federal court order mandating desegregation sent the black children of Russell to the previously white county schools for ten of their twelve years of public education (and in a curiously lopsided exchange, it brought the white children from the county to such inner-city schools as Byck for just two years). Many of the black children have come back, though, by means of medical excuses ("nerves") and fake addresses in white neighborhoods—Mrs. Carbin's two nephews included. "Busing took Byck away from us," she said. "I'm sorry we lost it." She stopped for a moment, looked up and winked. "But we don't feel like we did. It's still our school."

The busing order—handed down six weeks before the start of the 1975–76 school year—changed Byck overnight from almost 100 percent black to about 85 percent white. Students from Byck's neighborhood were sent to four outlying schools; and those schools, in turn, sent some of their children to Byck. The merger of the two school systems, which accompanied desegregation, meant the loss of Byck's rigidly prescribed instructional program and more than 60 of the school's specially funded aides and teachers. And so Byck faced the new school year with no set instructional materials, a large number of conservative, former county teachers who bitterly resented having been sent to the inner-city, and a student body representing a startlingly wide range of economic, racial, and cultural groups.

Chaos ensued. Each grade level ended up with a distinctly different way of grouping and teaching children. Teachers were supposed to rely on the county's educational television programs, but Byck had few TV sets. There was a lot less money for supplies, and there were no federal guidelines to tell the staff what to do with the little they had. Teachers began to take out their mounting frustrations in emotional meetings. But this turned out to be a "blessing in disguise," recalled Benningfield. "We were so involved in federal programs that we couldn't see the extent to which outside forces were controlling this school's life and had split us apart. Busing sent us scrambling. It all came back down to the teachers: cursing, sweating, showing their fists, working out their own problems."

A year later, their new-found independence led teachers voluntarily to increase the size of their classes to free the time of one of their peers, 28-year-old Mrs. Walker, whom they elected to serve as their instructional coordinator. A unique kind of school organization was born, one in which Mrs. Walker handles most of the school's internal affairs involving students while Benningfield takes care of Byck's external relationships with its communities and the school system. The arrangement has had its problems. Mrs. Walker is responsible for almost every aspect of Byck's instructional program, but she hasn't had the administrative power to evaluate teachers. Benningfield, who has that power, has been more apt to be concerned with one of his pet projects, such as a "sex stereotyping awareness" program. Neither of the two, then, has been monitoring classroom activities on a regular basis. But according to some teachers, this division of duties has held the school together through its tumultuous history. "We go to Janice first," said a third-grade teacher. "She's really running the school. Without her, we'd be in trouble. Teachers are really isolated so much of the day; there has to be a curriculum leader—someone to talk to. Benningfield's too busy."

During the first year of busing, Benningfield, indeed, was kept very busy, particularly at meetings of worried parents whose children attended the cluster of four schools feeding students to Byck. This was the only such intraschool group formed in a county where opposition to desegregation ran at a fever pitch. At these cluster meetings, Benningfield told parents he didn't have all the answers, that they would have to work together to find them. "Oh, you should have seen all their faces looking at me," he said, setting his jaw in a grim expression. "I didn't try to influence their feelings toward desegregation, only to lessen the trauma caused by their feelings."

Anti-busing demonstrations raged in Louisville the first day of busing; in the media, the city became another Boston, a national symbol of resistance to desegregation. But the biggest problem at Byck that first day of school was a traffic jam caused by the scores of parents who had followed the buses from their suburbs to make sure their children arrived at their new school safely. Many of the parents stayed that day, and they came back throughout the year as Benningfield put them to work in the school's classrooms. Membership in Byck's PTA soared; parents from the cluster's schools published a newsletter, stressing unity. "It was one of the greatest years you could possibly imagine," said Alma Wright, then president of the PTA and head of a community development organization in the Portland area, a low-income, white Appalachian neighborhood. Portland children came to Byck for the first time that year, along with those from more middle-class areas. "When you'd walk into that school, you wouldn't know where the people had come from as far as how they got along. There were really good human relations, and that made for a good learning atmosphere. It's because they didn't act stupid and pretend as though there weren't any problems. They faced up to the situation."

And no doubt because of this attitude, some parents soon were surprised to learn that Byck was far superior to the schools in their middle-class neighborhoods. David Hawpe, for instance, had lived in Boston during that city's first year of busing and so was "initially apprehensive" about sending his son, Christopher, away from his neighborhood, the St. Matthews area in the east end of the county. "Byck was a shock—it was really flourishing," he said. After Christopher's mandatory year at Byck, Hawpe was able to send him to his neighborhood school. But, he said, this quickly turned into "a disaster." By midyear, Christopher had lost ground in both reading and math, and he was losing interest in attending school. Hawpe went to see Benningfield and Mrs. Walker. "They were outraged," he said. "They took Christopher back in and salvaged that year. He got back up to his grade level and beyond."

Even those who remained deeply opposed to the idea of sending their children to school on Louisville's predominantly black west side appeared to appreciate Byck. Children from the Lowell School, which serves a white, working-class area in the southern part of the city where anti-busing feelings ran the highest, were added to Byck's cluster at the start of the 1979–80 school year. "The west end is strange to me; I wouldn't go down there at night," said Charmaine Hayden, as she waited in Lowell's parking lot for her second grader's bus to arrive from Byck. "Busing is useless. But if they have to go, I'm glad they're going to Byck. My kid is happier there, and I can't argue with that."

So in all quarters, Byck appears to have met the first challenge of desegregation: finding a way for parents—rich and poor, black and white—to get along well enough so their children can attend school together comfortably and with a minimum of distractions. But there is another, underlying challenge for desegregated schools: bridging the achievement gap between low-income and middle-class students. And whether Byck has met this second test—one that is beyond the influence of artful human relations—is perhaps best answered by a look at two fourth-grade classrooms.

* * *

The teacher was trying to explain to the fourth graders the meaning of the word *ecology*, but his own vocabulary problems and their seeming disinterest were taking the lesson nowhere. "Am I talking over your heads?" he asked at one point. "Do you know what I mean by effect? The ecology has an effect on the environment.

"Now look, slick!" he suddenly yelled, turning to a knot of bored kids over in the corner. Some were squirming painfully; a few were sleeping; one was playing with some chalk. "If you don't listen, I'm going to have to knock some heads together. . . . OK, it's time for Reading Plus," he added with a sigh of relief. "You hard-headed boys, let's line up."

All but 13 of the 31 children got in line to leave the room for Byck's specially funded reading program for those who are behind in their studies. There were no nonreaders in this class, but as a group the students were reading more like second graders than fourth graders. Almost all of the children came from two communities, the Russell and Portland areas, both low-income neighborhoods.

This was one of two fourth-grade classrooms at Byck; it might be called the "ghetto class." The other—the "suburban class"—was directly across the hall. In that room, the teacher was working with several children at her desk, while the rest of the class worked on its own. Some were doing their assignments for the day; others were looking up interesting topics in encyclopedias. "This is the Titanic," one student, the son of the PTA president, informed a visitor.

"Can I have your attention for a minute?" the teacher

quietly asked the children. "Your creative writing is on the board. 'One dark and rainy night, I was forced to stay in an old, creaking house.' Now finish that, will you please."

Of the 27 students in this class, most came from middle-class neighborhoods in the east end of Jefferson County. None needed to go to Byck's special reading program, and about half were reading close to the sixth-grade level. In nearly all respects, this class was everything the "ghetto class" was not. It is hard to accept that both were in the same school, let alone across the hall from each other.

Neither of the teachers in the two classrooms liked the way Byck's fourth graders had been split into two distinct groups according to students' achievement levels (and essentially by social classes, as well). They accurately referred to their classes as "two different worlds" and said the division was not helping either the low- or high-achieving students. As the teacher of the "suburban class," who might be expected to have been most pleased with the arrangement, put it: "A mixed class is a lot better for both groups—the lows have something to work towards, and the highs act so much better and aren't held back."

The teacher's impressions are supported by educational research on the effects of grouping children with others of similar ability (homogeneously) versus the effects of grouping children with varying abilities (heterogeneously). "We find that homogeneous ability grouping ... shows no consistent, positive value for helping students generally, and particular groups of students, to learn better," concluded an extensive review of the studies on ability grouping, published in 1971 by the Center for Educational Improvement at the University of Georgia. Nevertheless, the practice of assigning children to classes with other students of the same ability level remains widespread in America's public elementary schools, as a convenience for teachers and out of the mistaken belief that it makes for better instruction.

Another form of ability grouping, the "tracking" of students into certain courses or areas of study (such as vocational training) based on test scores or teacher evaluations, also remains common at the high school level. In schools that serve a mix of racial groups, both the use of homogeneous ability grouping and tracking can prevent classroom integration. White students are put in certain classes, blacks in others under the guise of serving different abilities. It's an effective technique to defeat the purpose of court-ordered desegregation plans, while still maintaining a semblance of compliance with the law by having the proper, overall mix of students within school buildings.

At Byck, homogeneous ability grouping did not quite result in racially segregated classrooms. Although the "ghetto" fourth-grade class had far more black students than the "suburban" class, Byck had enough low-income white students to provide a measure of racial balance within the "low-ability" group. More than racial segregation, the "ghetto class" represented socioeconomic segregation—not illegal, but an even more educationally damaging arrangement. Aware of this, some teachers said they argued against dividing the fourth grade into ability groups. But Benningfield, they said, insisted upon it in order to appease certain parents. He later denied this was so, explaining that his decision was based solely on the fact that there was an inordinately wide spread in abilities among Byck's fourth graders. But he also had divided the school's first grade intentionally; and this division clearly was along social-class lines, for the students did not have established achievement records upon which to base ability groups.

Byck's average achievement record was steadily improving in the late 1970s, drawing acclaim for the school. University of Indiana researchers, for instance, selected it in 1979 to be one of eight maverick schools in the Midwest to be studied as models of effective urban education. But the sharp differences between Byck's two fourth-grade class-rooms are an indication that there were decidedly separate groups of children within the school's relatively high, over-all achievement average. And each of the achievement records of these groups was not so praiseworthy as their composite. A random examination of the records of several dozen low-income white students from Portland and low-income black students from Russell showed they typically were held back in the first or second grades, while Byck's middle-class students advanced normally. Even more telling is what was happening to the Portland students later on in their school careers. They made up a third of Byck's enrollment, and were the only pupils to attend the school every year under the desegregation order; so, in a real sense, they were the best test of the school's effectiveness. The Portland students, however, were the vast majority of pupils enrolled in Byck's special reading program for low achievers. And when they left the school for junior high, they tended to be a year behind their grade level in reading.

For all the good feelings that parents in every one of its communities held towards Byck, then, it was an effective school primarily for the sons and daughters of the middle class. In essence, its achievement pattern simply mirrored the broader student achievement divisions evident along social class lines in school districts across the country. Byck was not interrupting the typical correlation between social class and achievement. And the separation of its first and fourth graders into different classrooms according to their social classes can only have been encouraging the achievement gap.

Benningfield agreed the "real test of a school is when you teach these [low-income] kids as well as any other. It's difficult, but not impossible. It's like surgery: Most any surgeon can take out an appendix, but brain surgery is where the going really gets tough." And in the fall of 1979, he apparently believed that Byck was not in need of any kind of operation. "I'm satisfied," he said, "that I'm serving both low- and high-end children. . . . You can't bring all kids to the top."

At least one Byck teacher, though, pointed to the school's homogeneously grouped classes as the evidence that Byck lacked the "push to do anything other than a reasonably good job." Said Tim Daly, a first-grade teacher: "We're good, but not an exceptional school. We hardly ever see the test scores for the kids. We just get all this soft stuff about feeling good from Benningfield." Some would suggest that unless Byck's parents apply pressure on the school's staff, Benningfield included, it will always be that way. But its low-income parents—no less than those in its middle-class neighborhoods—seemed as satisfied with Byck as Benningfield himself; his conscientious touch at human relations had taken care of that. In the absence of such a struggle for high achievement by all the school's students, the situation at Byck was summarized well (although unknowingly) by a 1979 University of Delaware report on effective schools: "By concentrating his efforts on good community relations and positive student attitudes towards themselves and the school, a principal can become wellliked, look busy and have a happy, humming school. The students and their parents will lose in the end, but they probably will not realize the principal's neglect in their failure to achieve."

In the end, though, the problem faced by Byck's lowincome parents was far more complex, far more practical than theoretical. Although Benningfield may have defused them with loving care, there also was no alternative for them in Louisville better than Byck. Portland parents, for instance, often compared Byck to the nearby Roosevelt School, and they said Roosevelt was the last place they'd send their children. "Byck is so much better," said Charles Wade, the father of a first grader. "The kids act right there." And Russell area's black children were not faring well in the county's predominantly white schools, often ending up labeled as "learning disabled." They would come back to Byck, and their school records showed they'd start learning again. "The entire school system is a mess," said a black father of four, standing outside Byck. "I'm trying to get one of mine in this school. This is a good school, compared to the others."

* * *

Like the Edison School in Michigan, Byck has never been a static world. Matt Benningfield's style of leadership and the continual challenges thrust upon it from outside have seen to that. But in contrast to Edison, Byck is no dinosaur; its staff seems to have found ways to flow with, if not thrive on, changes—to evolve in response to shifts in the school's environment. And in the spring of 1980, the changes at Byck continued. For instance, the teacher of the fourth-grade "ghetto class" was dismissed by the school system—not because of ineffective teaching, but amid parents' charges that he was molesting children (which later led to indictments). On a more positive note, the school's average achievement scores hit a new high. At the same time, Jefferson County's desegregation plan was altered so that Byck would receive fewer middle-class pupils and more students from the Portland area, making the issue of the school's effectiveness with low-income children even more critical. And on this score, an in-depth newspaper report detailing Byck's successes and its problems prompted Tim Daly and Janice Walker to organize a half-dozen after-school meetings attended by eight to ten teachers and Benningfield.

The meetings were akin to the Weight Watchers type of self-help sessions recommended by Michigan State school climate researchers Wilbur Brookover and Lawrence Lezotte; it was not an unusual activity, though, for a school where communication has been the byword. The group of teachers called itself an "Exceptional School Planning Committee," and its goal was to address the academic disparities among Byck's students. As Daly put it: "If we were going to be perceived as an exceptional school—whether that's true or not—we desired to be so in an academic sense, not simply because everyone likes us. So we invited all teachers to participate in the meetings and told them we were going to decide on a new direction in which to go. We told them if they didn't participate and didn't agree with our decisions, they could always leave the school."

Despite the group's lofty aims, it quickly got bogged down in the problem of how to design a proper system to evaluate the school's effectiveness with all its students— within each grade, classroom, social class, and racial group. Although this could be a relatively simple matter, it was compounded by Byck's built-in, 80 percent mobility rate from the desegregation plan alone. "The school district's testing people said they couldn't provide us with the information the way we wanted it," said Daly. "Another problem was that some teachers feared a detailed evaluation system could be misused as a weapon against them, particularly if the school's present leaders ever left." The group also discussed both mastery learning and DISTAR, but some teachers recalled negative experiences with Byck's rigidly structured "behavior analysis" program in the early 1970s and did not want to return to any similar kind of system. "We didn't want to try something because someone else said it worked, but because we thought it would work," said Daly. And so the committee ended the 1979–80 school year without making any substantive decisions, except one—to discontinue grouping students homogeneously.

Mrs. Walker said she had high hopes for the committee continuing in the 1980–81 school year and perhaps making some firm decisions. Daly said he had similar hopes, but he was more skeptical about the group's potential, believing that Benningfield viewed the sessions merely as "in-service training rather than trying to make fundamental changes." Benningfield, though, was singing a different tune in many respects. "I have never really been totally satisfied at any single point with the way things are here," he said. "We can always do better." He said he intended to spend more time in Byck's classrooms monitoring instruction and to conduct more training sessions for teachers. And he, too, wanted the committee to continue working: "I see this group as a way for us to become very aware of what we're doing with all children, as a way for us to self-adjust quickly in mid-flight. We have to be able to examine very carefully what we're doing in each classroom. We have to know what skills the children are weak in, and why. And we have to be able to do something about it—not in a year or a half-year, but within days. I'm willing to do it."

Looking At Your School: Desegregation

In the quarter century since the U.S. Supreme Court's historic *Brown v. Board of Education* decision outlawing segregated schools, desegregation has been the most volatile, frustrating issue in American public education. The dilemma has grown more subtle as the battleground for equal rights has shifted from the dual school systems of the South to the urban centers of the North, where black students now are often in the majority. The critical legal distinction between *de jure* (by government action) and *de facto* (by private decisions) segregation has complicated and slowed the drive to diminish racial isolation in northern public schools. There has been increasing confusion, too, about the social and educational effects of desegregation. However, the constitutional and moral imperative remains clear and unaltered: Separate facilities for black and white students are inherently unequal.

"Busing" has been the code word, and fear of it gave sudden rise to "neighborhood school" policies in many cities. A common tactic of northern school boards has been to call for "quality, integrated" education and, at the same time, to promote neighborhood schools, which unavoidably are based on racially segregated housing. Although various attempts have been made to justify neighborhood schools as something of a national tradition or recognized right, this is a myth. Public education began hundreds of years ago in this country, while neighborhood schools developed only in the twentieth century as a byproduct of the growth of large cities. Even in school districts holding closely to neighborhood school policies, the number of these schools decreased in the 1970s. With declining enrollments and a growing recognition that schools should be large enough to offer varied educational opportunities, districts in both urban and rural areas have been consolidating schools and closing many neighborhood facilities. Another trend, the creation of magnet schools, has put many more children on the bus.

Transporting students—"busing"—has been part of public education for more than 100 years, ever since Massachusetts began hiring farmers to take children to school in wagons. States and school boards regularly vote funds for this purpose, often providing free transportation to any child who lives more than a mile or two from his school. In 1972, a study by the Metropolitan Applied Research Center estimated that if every student in the nation were transported for the sole purpose of integrating schools, the number riding buses to school would not increase and might even decrease. And so in a nation where millions of children already ride the bus each day, where neighborhood schools have been on the decline, and where one of five families moves each year anyway, the veneration of neighborhood schools and the attendant fear of busing seem to shield deeper levels of opposition to desegregation.

As some black parents have suggested, the real problem may be "not the bus, but us." It would be a mistake to assume that outright racial prejudice does not exist any longer in America; rooting it out remains unfinished business in every region of the country. However, there are some indications that this may not be the issue it once was. A 1979 poll, commissioned by the National Conference of Christians and Jews, found racial animosity decreasing. Only 37 percent of whites surveyed said they felt blacks were trying to "move too fast"—down 34 percentage points from 1966. Sizeable majorities of whites favored affirmative action programs for blacks in industry and education. Whites who said they would be upset if blacks moved into their neighborhood declined from 62 percent in 1963 to 39 percent. A critical finding of the study was that, among parents whose children are bused, only 8 percent of the blacks and 16 percent of the whites said the experience was unsatisfactory; the most common reaction was, "There are just no problems, no complaints from the children."

Classroom observations at Byck and many other integrated schools confirm the findings of this study. If the issue of race were to be tried before a jury of school children, chances are they would find the evidence boring. "As long as you go to school and learn something and don't fight and don't sit around and say who's this and who's that, as long as you're trying to get something for yourself—that's what's important," said an eighth grader, voicing the prevailing attitude among students. At the elementary school level, racial problems are rare in integrated schools. Younger children simply are not that conscious of color; if allowed, they make friends and scatter about their classes and playgrounds irrespective of race. "When you do get something racial," said the principal of an integrated, inner-city elementary, "it's nearly always been ground into their heads by someone or something, usually a parent." Racial attitudes, however, harden when black and white students are kept isolated from each other, a common situation at the elementary school level. "They build up these clichés," said a black teacher at a nearly all-white elementary school. To demonstrate, she asked her class what they know about black people, and a student responded: "They got big lips—big Afros." Such attitudes, born in isolation and allowed to go unchallenged, quickly spawn rigid patterns of interaction at the high school level, where many students encounter others of a different race for the first time. But even then, self-segregation—rather than fighting or overt tension—remains the most common reaction. Black and white high-school students who are not comfortable with each other may go their own way, not eat together or share many interests in common, but they are rarely at each other's throats. That usually occurs only with the prodding of the larger community of adults.

So, transporting students away from their neighborhoods and having them get along reasonably well once at school is not an unworkable, unattainable goal. But there is another, perhaps even more difficult challenge involved in desegregation—an educational struggle. White parents fear sending their children to black schools because they believe these schools are inferior; and quite often, their perceptions are all too accurate. Of course, this is only true to the extent that blacks tend to be poorer than whites and that schools attended by poorer students tend to be worse than those attended by middle-class children. Good schools and students, either black or white, ease much of the resistance to desegregation; bad schools and students, either black or white, provide one more set of excuses for not mixing students. As Muriel Carrison noted, in a paper presented before the American Psychological Association in 1977: "Would anyone seriously object if the son or daughter of a black with five Ph.D.s and three Nobel Prizes enrolled in Beverly Hills? No—it's the children of the poor that we fear." Conversely, truly excellent schools in low-income, black neighborhoods, such as the Beasley Academic Center in Chicago, are proving to be one of the few ways to draw middle-class white students voluntarily to the inner city. So although race would seem to be the critical issue in desegregation, the basic educational problem, to the extent that blacks tend to be poorer than whites, boils down to the tough task of reforming schools so that all children—from both low- and middle-income families—are served well. Viewed in this light, the challenge of desegregation comes right back to the central question of this book: How can the achievement gap between low-income and middle-class students be bridged?

Historically, many school districts have avoided meeting the educational challenge posed by desegregation by integrating black students with poor whites, creating even greater concentrations of low-income students with even greater instructional problems. Separating children by ability grouping and tracking has been another way to dodge reform and maintain the achievement differential. Since socioeconomic segregation is not prohibited by the federal Constitution, desegregation carried out in this manner is generally within the law. But it is nothing more than an educational hoax. And the prevalence of such economically segregated, but racially integrated schools may be one of the reasons why studies on the effects of desegregation have not shown conclusively that it improves the achievement of black students in and of itself. When achievement gains among black students have been reported, many researchers believe the results reflect two additional factors:

socioeconomic integration and instruction improvements, specifically those techniques proven to have been most effective with low-income students. "Desegregation won't accomplish anything by itself," said Daniel Levine, director of the Center for the Study of Metropolitan Problems in Education at the University of Missouri at Kansas City. "If you ignore quality education, desegregation will be sabotaged. Many of the problems of desegregation go back to the problem that we still don't know how to teach very well, that better instructional methods need to be emphasized."

In the 1970s, the courts demonstrated a growing appreciation for the necessity of tying desegregation to efforts to improve the achievement of low-income students. Although judges avoided defining "effective" instruction in the context of educational malpractice suits, mandated "educational components" increasingly were included in court-ordered desegregation plans. A major reason for this legal development is that most desegregation orders have been limited to central cities; with certain exceptions (Louisville and Wilmington, Delaware), white suburban districts have been allowed to remain outside urban desegregation plans. The result is that, even with court-ordered desegregation, black students in many cities remain in the majority in their schools. And so it has become clear that simply moving bodies—say, busing a black child from a 90 percent black school to a 70 percent black school—would have limited benefit. The courts, then, have looked to other, educational means to address the past effects of segregation.

According to Levine, this trend was foreshadowed in the Denver desegregation case in 1971 and emerged unmistakably in court decisions in Boston and Detroit between 1974 and 1976. In Boston, for example, the federal judge literally took over South Boston High, appointing a new headmaster to insure that his desegregation order would be carried out faithfully. In Detroit, Judge Robert DeMascio Jr. ordered comprehensive compensatory education, teacher training, testing, and counseling programs for every school, and he directed the state of Michigan to pay half the cost. The U.S. Supreme Court upheld DeMascio's ruling in 1977 affirming that court-ordered desegregation could go beyond mere student reassignment. Since then, the role of such ancillary relief blossomed even more fully in at least two other desegregation cases, neither fully resolved by the fall of 1980.

In the first case, Judge Noel Fox had ordered the Kalamazoo, Michigan, schools to desegregate in 1973. When two court-appointed experts reported on the school system's compliance with his order in 1979, however, he learned that it had done a good job of moving children around, but it was not providing equal educational opportunities within its classrooms. Specifically citing increased disparities between black and white students in basic skills achievement, the outside evaluators found that the district's academic programs remained segregated, beginning at the elementary school level. Ability grouping was used in about half of Kalamazoo's elementary classrooms and tracking was common in its junior and senior highs. Elementary-school special and compensatory education programs and upper-grade remedial and noncollege preparatory programs had disproportionate numbers of black students, and students in these programs were falling further behind rather than catching up. Fox adopted the experts' recommendations, essentially ordering Kalamazoo to develop a districtwide mastery learning approach. His order, under appeal in 1980, called for the schools to develop a common set of goals, objectives, expectations, and curricula for all students in the basic skills, beginning with kindergarten; create compensatory education programs to mainstream students in remedial programs back into regular classes; monitor students' progress more closely so that learning problems could be corrected immediately; and eventually discard ability groups and tracking.

As detailed as Fox's instructional orders were, the San Diego desegregation case led to even more specific educational mandates. In this case, a three-year-old voluntary desegregation plan that had not worked, as well as foot-dragging by school administrators in assuming responsibility for the achievement of all students, brought a remarkably determined Superior Court of California judge to some new frontiers for judicial involvement in instructional matters. Operating under the broad powers of California law, which makes no distinction between *de jure* and *de facto* segregation, Judge Louis Welch, in the fall of 1980, was about to order the San Diego school board to revise its curriculum with the goal of bringing at least 70 percent of the students in the school district's racially isolated, low-achieving schools up to national norms on achievement tests by the 1983–84 school year.

As in the Kalamazoo case, the judge's stance was based primarily on a scathing report by a team of outside examiners, although he also had taken the unusual step of sitting in San Diego's classrooms himself. The team—which included Joseph Rosen, the retired superintendent of Chicago's District 10, where DISTAR was used widely in the mid-1970s—specifically looked at 23 San Diego schools that had inordinately high percentages of black and Hispanic students and very low achievement levels, averaging some 30 percentage points below the district as a whole. The team's strongly worded report was nothing less than a state-of-the-art summary of how to improve the quality of education at low-income schools. Its recommendations included: Principals must serve as instructional leaders, be evaluated in terms of students' performance, and retain their jobs on the basis of meeting established achievement goals; responsibility for achievement should be returned to regular classroom teachers, instead of relying heavily on a range of fragmented special programs that pull children out of their regular classes; student testing should be tied directly to instructional efforts to correct deficiencies; schoolwide homework policies should be adopted and strictly followed; and more emphasis should be put on improving students' attendance.

According to local observers, San Diego school officials, who had been maintaining that low student achievement was the product of socioeconomic factors beyond their control, simply panicked when Welch ordered them to respond to the report. For one reason, school officials feared that the judge might order them to use DISTAR in many of their schools. Its limited use in San Diego already had stirred political controversy within the school system. However, Welch had been talking by phone with Siegfried Engelmann, DISTAR's creator; and the judge clearly was impressed with the program's record, making such statements from the bench as, "Those high up in the universities, in the towers, who hardly ever soil their hands teaching children, don't like it. But those in the pits do." So the board hastily brought in Walter Thompson from the May School in Chicago to tell them about mastery learning. Then, in the summer of 1980, the board announced it would expand its use of DISTAR to about 40 San Diego classrooms, but it would use its own mastery learning program at 17 of the 23 racially isolated schools—a program based on the concepts of both DISTAR and the Chicago mastery learning materials. This plan, school officials said, would raise students' achievement 9 percent in three years.

The board's achievement goals immediately were criticized as far too modest. And in a rare moment of agreement, both Engelmann and Michael Katims, developer of the Chicago program, publicly attacked the San Diego mastery learning program, saying it was ill-conceived, misrepresented their ideas, and would not work because it was based on a traditional basal reader. The board then selected an outside evaluator, Sidney Estes, superintendent of instruction for the Atlanta, Georgia, schools. But Estes even was skeptical of the board's proposed program, noting that it carried most of the glaring defects of the district's existing instructional programs: insufficient training, lack of coordination, lack of central control, and insufficient monitoring and evaluation of principals and teachers.

In a "memorandum of intended decision," released September 8, 1980, Welch, too, blasted San Diego school officials, accusing them of a "lack of candor" and of "twisting facts to win a case." Specifically citing the successes of DISTAR in East St. Louis, Illinois, and in Mt. Vernon, New York, of phonics-based programs in other cities, and of certain maverick schools in the "abysmal ghettos" of New York and Chicago, he wrote: "If positive outcomes are possible there, how much easier it should be to produce noteworthy results in South East San Diego [a racially isolated, low-income area] where the physical, social and psychological environment is relatively uplifting in comparison. The court will accept no less than that which has been achieved elsewhere." To this end, Welch listed 24 orders that were likely to be included in his actual decision. They included the goal of bringing at least 70 percent of the students in the district's racially isolated, low-achieving schools up to their grade levels within four years; continuously evaluating all district staff, from teachers to the superintendent; hiring a court-approved consultant to study the district's fragmented administrative structure; exploring the possibility of pay incentives to attract and retain effective principals and teachers in low-achieving schools; establishing full-day kindergartens at each of the racially isolated schools; promoting students only after they had mastered the lessons at each grade level; and minimizing the loss of instructional time in the basic skills due to uncoordinated programs.

Welch still was willing to leave the choice of a specific instructional program to accomplish these goals up to school officials, but he also made it clear that he would hold all of them responsible for producing gains in student achievement, starting with school Superintendent Thomas Goodman: "Systems such as DISTAR, mastery learning, Open Court [a phonics-based program] and others have value only insofar as they are properly prepared, coordinated, implemented and monitored. The test of the district's proposed program will be in students' achievements. The court hopes it will succeed. It can if some fundamental changes are made—*now!* The program cannot be directed by a committee. The board must require the person at the top to follow through or find someone else who will." And he warned that if another year passed without significant progress, he would administer the district's academic programs himself.

As advanced as Welch's actions in San Diego have been in bringing educational issues to the forefront of a desegregation case, a caveat should be entered here: While he was attempting to force the school system to launch a serious effort to improve the quality of education it was providing at its lowest-achieving schools, he also appeared content to allow these schools to remain racially isolated. "No one here wants busing—not the judge, not even most black leaders," said a close observer of the case. And so in San Diego, it seems that a push for quality education has overridden the longstanding legal doctrine that "separate is inherently unequal." It is a regressive tradeoff, even if it originates with some progressive thinking about the nature of the desegregation problem. Desegregation cannot work well without instructional reforms, but these reforms are not a substitute for desegregation. Equal educational opportunity in the 1980s requires both.

7

The Fourth R— Responsibility: *The Modesto Plan*

I t is time to admit it: In the last dozen years, educators have made a mess of things. The evidence against us is overwhelming. When children are safer on the streets than in their schools, when we are spending more on vandalism than on textbooks, and when we are clothing functional illiterates in caps and gowns, the time has come to start plea bargaining. We are guilty.

James C. Enochs, 1979
The Restoration of Standards

The trappings of Jim Enochs's office tell much of the story—the story of an educator with the guts to wake up to the best-kept secret in America's public schools: "Kids want adults to act like adults. They want to know who's in charge. They want to know what's expected of them. They want to know what's right and wrong today will be right and wrong tomorrow."

Thirteen large posters crowd the wall directly across from Enochs's desk; in simple language, they outline the basic academic skills that all of the 20,000 students in the public schools of Modesto, California, are expected to master at every grade level. Between his office windows hang two homemade charts showing changes in the achievement test scores of the city's students since 1976; the lines connecting their reading and math marks rise steeply, like mountains from a valley.

A plaque behind his desk declares: "Eagles Don't Flock." And a framed cartoon on the same wall portrays Moses leading his followers across the Red Sea, with a clear path ahead and towering waves threatening on both sides. "Of course it's damp underfoot," reads the caption below, "that strikes me as a very petty complaint to make at a time like this."

Enochs's open briefcase rests on a nearby chair; a handful of brightly colored pamphlets spills out. Together, they clearly detail an interlocking set of student, teacher, and parent responsibilities for conduct, basic skills performance, homework, testing, and meeting graduation requirements. Among the papers atop his desk are several sheets bearing the school system's bold letterhead: "Our Fourth R is Responsibility," it states.

Enoch no doubt is conscious of the cumulative effect of these adornments. The impression is intentional, the cultivated display of a man who is sure he is right. From every angle, there is little uncertainty about the message: *accountability.* The public schools hold Modesto's students to certain standards, and Modesto can hold its public schools—and itself—responsible for how its children measure up to these standards.

It is just that simple, but it is also a public covenant which few cities—large or small—can begin to claim. The product of a straightforward stance, it sets Enochs far apart from his fellow educators, those entrusted with running this nation's public schools. His efforts as assistant superintendent of Modesto's schools exemplify what educational leadership can accomplish in a situation crying for someone to take charge. Although Modesto is a medium-sized, solidly middle-class school district, the various elements of Enochs's "Fourth R" plan to restore educational standards here mirror many of the findings of this nationwide search for what makes schools work well in far more desperate, urban settings. His plan represents a comprehensive approach to infusing the classrooms of an entire city with the kind of clear-cut and closely-held sense of responsibility that typically accounts for the successes of maverick schools. And its results suggest that the path to good schools is not all that different whether it's in the South Bronx, the south side of Chicago, or this placid community on the West Coast.

* * *

In 1975, when Jim Enochs was promoted from high-school principal to head of curriculum and instruction for the Modesto schools, there was no great hue and cry about the achievement of the city's students. Surrounded by miles of irrigated fruit farms, Modesto is a conservative, fast-growing city of slightly more than 100,000 residents. It sits on a flat, brown plain in the heart of the world's richest agricultural area, the San Joaquin Valley, about 90 miles east of San Francisco and approximately the same distance south of Sacramento. "Water, wealth, contentment, health," boasts the permanent sign arching over one of the city's downtown streets. True to the slogan, peaches, nuts, apricots, and wine-making have provided Modesto with a relatively stable economic base. As might be expected, its schools never have had many of the nagging problems that afflict larger, more urban districts. And its children—predominantly white and well off—have never slipped that far below national achievement standards.

But Enochs did not become a school administrator to maintain the status quo or, as he put it, "to join the Rotary Club." Instead, he took a long look at what was happening in the public schools across the nation: the plummeting achievement, the rising disruption and conflict, the public's growing concern and unwillingness to provide financial support to an apparently shaky enterprise. He figured there was "no reason to believe that Modesto will be exempt from either the problem or the reaction." And he decided to act early to prevent the crisis.

The heart of the public schools' problems, as Enochs analyzed it, was not the students themselves nor dislocations in society, but educators' failure to uphold their professional responsibilities. "In the name of innovation and relevancy, we suspended our better judgment," he later wrote in *The Restoration of Standards*, a pamphlet published in 1979 by the Phi Delta Kappa Educational Foundation, a national educators' society. "Rather than be thought rigid in a period when flexibility was the highest virture, we first relaxed our standards and then abolished them completely. We began to feel guilty and proceeded to pull up our roots and examine them for rot. Homework, honest grading, demanding courses, required courses, earned promotion—up they went and out they went. We leveled the field so that all could pass through without labor or frustration. . . . To be sure, we have had our share of accomplices . . . pop psychologists who convinced us that grades were responsible for everything from bed-wetting to the military/industrial complex; social engineers who turned schools into battering rams for their latest experiments; and innovation hustlers with hardware, software and a copy of the latest Elementary-Secondary Act funding proposal. . . .

"But there was an even more appealing element in their siren call, a kind of hidden melody that we could never publicly acknowledge: It was all simply easier that way. If there were no standardized bench marks against which to be measured, there was no accountability. The tough, time-consuming process of monitoring—teachers monitoring students, principals monitoring teachers, superintendents monitoring principals—was lifted from our shoulders. There were fewer decisions to be made, judgments to be weighed, and stands to be taken. Yes is always easier to say than no. Something called the 'affective domain' became the cloak of decency for lazy teachers and administrators. It was easier to make students feel good than to hold them accountable to the rigors of learning."

So without federal funds or a study committee, Enochs set out on his own to develop what he later called a "modest proposal to get back on the high road from which we strayed in the mid-1960s, to do what we're supposed to do—educate kids." In April 1976, after a year of 16-hour-workdays, he brought before the Modesto school board eight unambiguous principles, the foundation of his "Fourth R" program. The principles were:

• It is essential that a public institution clearly define itself, say unequivocally what it believes in and stands for.

• The development of responsible adults is a task requiring community involvement. It cannot be left solely to the public schools.

• The principal tasks of the public schools cannot be achieved if a disproportionate amount of time and resources must be given to maintaining order.

• Parents must consistently support the proposition that students have responsibilities as well as rights, and the schools have an obligation to insist upon both.

• High performance takes place in a framework of high expectations; standards without rewards and consequences are not standards at all.

• The full responsibility for learning cannot be transferred from the student to the teacher.

• There is nothing inherently undemocratic in requiring students to do things that are demonstrably beneficial to them.

• In order for a program to succeed, it must be maintained for a reasonable period of time and be assured of continued support.

Nailing these principles to the schoolhouse doors in Modesto was an ambitious step: "Our scaled-down version of the 95 Theses nailed to the door of the Wittenberg Church by Martin Luther," Enochs proclaimed. His purpose, though, was not public relations; he intended to take the school board further than mere paper promises. Attached to each of the eight principles were detailed programs designed to bring them to life in every one of the city's classrooms. The programs were:

• A basic skills, minimum competency plan for grades kindergarten through eight. The minimum levels were stated in terms of specific skills and knowledge—rather than the arcane language of test scores—so that every parent could readily understand them. Students were to be tested twice yearly. All were to be screened initially at midyear by a standardized test; those who scored below grade level were to take a year-end, criterion-referenced test. Failing this second test, a student could only be promoted if his teacher presented substantial classroom work demonstrating performance above the minimum level. The competency levels were but a floor, the lowest acceptable performance that would earn promotion.

• In Modesto's high schools, a graduation plan based on minimum-competency, criterion-referenced tests in five areas: English (both reading and writing), math, social studies, science, and health. These tests were to be taken by all students in their junior year. Failure in any area would mean students would have to take a remedial course; no student would be granted a diploma without passing the tests in every subject.

• Beginning with grade four, annual assessments of students' writing abilities, again based on minimum skill levels established for each grade. Enochs brought in a trainer from the successful Bay Area Writing Project to show teachers and principals how to monitor students' writing by the "holistic" grading method (in which both the mechanics and the total effectiveness of the piece of writing are evaluated). Teachers had to begin filing quarterly reports with their principals showing the frequency and nature of their writing assignments; the principals, in turn, had to certify these reports to Enochs, who took home stacks of student compositions to read and then fired off notes to the teachers.

• Written conduct codes for both the elementary level and grades seven through twelve. These state specifically students' rights, responsibilities, and consequences resulting from the first and repeated infractions of school rules. As with the minimum competency requirements for each grade, handbooks outlining these codes were distributed to every student; parents had to sign a receipt verifying they had received the handbooks from their children.

• In grades kindergarten through six, a "character education" program taking up a half-hour of class time three days a week. This reflected neither a fascination with "values clarification" nor a heavy-handed effort to indoctrinate children in a rigid code of ethics. Instead, its purpose was to underscore commonly shared values, such as courage, kindness, honesty, and justice. "While it was once possible to assume that most students brought certain shared values with them to school," Enochs later wrote, "it is no longer so. If we expect the reflection of certain values in students' behaviors, we must be certain that they have been exposed to these values."

• A citizenship program for grades seven through twelve, in which each teacher would assign a quarterly mark to every student for being on time, meeting deadlines, and coming to class prepared. Two or more unsatisfactory marks would end certain privileges; students could regain these if they improved their marks the next quarter.

• A communitywide consortium on the problems of youth that would bring the schools into a closer working relationship with health, welfare, police, and court agencies.

Since first introducing these programs in 1976, Enochs added three more related elements to his plan:

• A community awards program, sponsored by corporations and institutions, to provide honors and incentives for students who excel in academics and citizenship at all grade levels.

• A "Help Yourself at Home and School" program in which clerks at each school give out prepared packets of homework assignments to students in need of extra work. Parents would be asked to sign "contracts" to enroll their children in the program, indicating they will provide a quiet time for the student to do his work at home, check the work and sign it each night.

• Devoting some of the district's federal funds for low-income, low-achieving students to retraining principals and teachers. Principals were expected to become "curriculum leaders who know good teaching when they see it and tolerate nothing less." (Enochs began evaluating his principals much more in terms of the performance of their students, although he had not yet made their jobs contingent on meeting certain established achievement goals.) And about 250 Modesto teachers have been trained to use DISTAR in their classes. (Enochs probably was one of the few school administrators in the country to act upon the results of the federal Follow Through study.)

Together all the elements of Enochs's "Fourth R" plan were meant "to place some pressure on everyone involved," he said. "We said to parents, 'You have the right to come to us and say, What will my kid know by the third grade, and how will I know that he knows it?' And we said to our employees, 'Here are the tools. Excuses are no longer valid.' " As he put it in *The Restoration of Standards*, the message was:

"This is our program.

"This is what we expect in behavior and academic performance.

"This is what happens to those who meet our standards.

"This is what happens to those who fail to meet our standards.

"At mid-year we'll tell you how we are doing.

"At the end of the year, we'll tell you how we did, as a district and at each school.

"These are the people who are in charge, at the district level and at each school."

It meant substituting a system of mutual accountability and rewards, a common civic thrust, for what Enochs called "the circle of irresponsibility," the endless finger-pointing that characterizes public education. Although it meant increased responsibilities for all concerned, Enochs's plan prompted surprisingly little public reaction in Modesto, let alone resistance. He did have to back away from a group of right-wing religious fundamentalists who mistakenly assumed that he was in agreement with their beliefs. And after proposing the consortium of local agencies concerned with youth—hardly the most sweeping of his programs—he immediately was attacked by a county human-services administrator for implying that other organizations were not doing their jobs.

But the Modesto school board only needed a bit of prodding from Enochs to accept nearly all the elements of his plan right away. (The "character education" lessons drew the least initial support.) Even as many of its new members came to be elected with the backing of the district's teachers' union, the board has stood by its commitment to the "Fourth R"—despite budget cutbacks in the wake of California's Proposition 13 and through a bitter, seven-day teachers' strike in early 1980. If a more militant mood has arisen among Modesto's teachers, Enochs's plan has not been the source of it. As Carol Smith, a second-grade teacher and the strike chairman at Modesto's Marshal Elementary, said about two months before teachers walked off their jobs: "Enochs put teeth in what we're trying to do in the classroom. Now there's no haziness. We know our responsibilities and roles. It's good for us to be accountable; it's necessary for our credibility."

Modesto's parents have simply remained silent, except on two occasions. The first was in the fall of 1979, when about 20 athletes at a middle-class high school were kicked off their teams for receiving low citizenship marks; the board stood firm in the face of parent protests. And the second was in June 1980, when about 5 percent of the first graduating class required to meet the new graduation standards were told they would not receive their diplomas because they had failed at least one of the high-school-level competency tests twice. In this instance, the board caved in, angering Enochs. It decided to make an exception— "just for this first class"—and allow the students to take the tests a third time. (About two-thirds of them still failed, and those who wanted their diplomas had to go to night school.)

"We only hear from the community when something goes wrong," said Enochs, "otherwise we're left with grim encouragement." So the lack of vocal support for his "Fourth R" plan should not imply that it hasn't led to some favorable short-term results. On California's annual assessment tests, Modesto's third, sixth, and twelfth graders scored an average of 10 to 38 percentage points higher in reading, writing, spelling, and math in 1979 than they did in 1976, the year before the "Fourth R" plan was introduced. And on a national, standardized achievement test, almost 80 percent of the city's students in grades one through eight ranked at or above their grade levels in 1980, up about 15 percent in three years. But perhaps the most dramatic changes have been charted by the annual decreases in the percentages of students failing the district's new competency tests. For example, more than half of Modesto's ninth graders failed the math competency test in 1978, the first year it was administered to them; the next year, the percentage dropped to 15 percent among the same students. In reading, the percentage of failures fell from 12 to just 3 percent. And in writing, it dropped from 21 to 13 percent.

Within these averages, though, problems remained. Sixth graders at several low-income, predominantly black and Hispanic elementary schools in Modesto continued to lag more than a year behind their grade level. However, the district's Title I (low-income, low-achieving) schools, as a group, improved their average scores on the standardized test in 1980 at a more rapid rate than the district's middle-class elementaries. With the growing use of DISTAR in Modesto, close to half the students at some of the city's low-income schools were at or above their grade levels.

Enochs agrees that his "Fourth R" plan has not cured all of his public school system's ills. "I don't think we're through by any means," he said, "but we're on the right track. One of the problems in convincing people to hang tough on reform is they expect you to clean up a mess which accumulated over 10 years in just two or three. Happily, though, I do think we've begun to get over the 1960s, to get back to what education is all about."

* * *

Jim Enochs is not the kind of person usually found in a position of leadership in America's public school systems. He is well-read, particularly in fields outside of education. And he writes well, forsaking educators' impenetrable jargon which turns buses into "mobile learning modules" and field trips into "experiential interfacing with the environment." He seems truly to enjoy what he is doing, to be more interested in substance than form. Modesto's superintendent retired at the end of 1980; Enochs did not even apply for the job. "I think the best slot is Number Two," he said. "That's where the action is—curriculum, instruction, discipline. Politics and ass-kissing are not for me." He is a be-

liever in hard work, in the possibilities of human and institutional renewal. Unlike many of his colleagues, he does
not pander to the public's whims. And if he is not
popular—if he is viewed by some as an egotistical
moralist—he also is refreshingly honest about the necessity
for authority and the failings of those whose first response is
to pass the buck. "Someone has to decide," he said.
"There's no way around it."

Enochs was born in Southern California; his family
moved to Modesto when he was in the sixth grade. He went
to a local junior college, graduated from San Jose State, and
in the early 1960s entered a Ph.D. program in history at the
University of Colorado. He left there without a degree
when a new set of conservative regents undertook a political purge of his department; he summarizes that experience
by quoting the poet E. E. Cummings, "There are certain
kinds of shit I will not eat." Back in Modesto, that attitude
served him well through 12 years of teaching, a term as
president of the local teachers' union, and a period of criti-
cism for being among the early supporters of Cesar
Chavez's efforts to unionize area farmworkers. "There are
few things more demoralizing than serving an institution
which mocks one's highest personal values," he later wrote.
"It transforms initiative into impotence and dedication into
resignation. It turns professionals who care about their
clients into clock-punchers who care only about themselves." And so he turned to school administration, he said,
"because it didn't make a bit of difference what I was doing
in the classroom with 150 kids when all of this other crap
was going on in the outside world. I was attracted by the
leverage, the possibility of making a difference." In all this,
he cites his father—"an American original"—as the greatest
influence on him. "He was a totally disabled World War I
vet," Enochs said. "When he saw crap, he called it for what
it was. He used to regularly get out the typewriter and send
letters to Roosevelt and J. Edgar Hoover, telling them what

they should be doing. The man had an infallible bullshit detector."

With this in mind, Enochs would be the first to admit there's nothing particularly new in his "Fourth R" plan. What is unique is that he had the temerity to attempt to clearly define the purpose of his school system, to outline a total plan to accomplish that purpose and to expect everyone involved to live by it. As a package, there is nothing so completely stated within the broad sweep of American education, where definitions are often obscured by qualifications, responsibilities are often no more than hollow words, and cross-purposes are a way of life.

The underlying principles of Enochs's plan so impressed the Rev. Jesse Jackson, the charismatic and vocal leader of the Chicago-based People United to Save Humanity organization, that he adopted a similar platform for his "PUSH for Excellence" high schools. Enochs admires Jackson "as the one national black figure that's not handing out that tired old liberal stuff about 'it's all because of the kids' environment.'" But at the same time he is repelled by Jackson because his programs invariably have been poorly managed and too dependent on his inspiring presence. A 1980 report by the National Institute of Education came to a similar conclusion, terming PUSH-Excel more of a "movement" than an educational program. Following this critical review, Jackson called upon Enochs once more, bringing him to Chicago in the summer, 1980, to begin work on specific programs by which PUSH-Excel could fulfill its many promises.

In part because of Jackson, Enochs's plan began to attract nationwide attention in the late 1970s. Invitations to address his peers and hundreds of requests for more information poured in—all of which have taught Enochs some lessons about the sad state of leadership in America's public schools. "It seemed pretentious to advance my plan as anything special," he said. "But then I discovered that most administrators have no idea what they're supposed to be doing. There's no magic. All it takes is the commitment, the time and the guts to stay with it. But few people really want to work at it. Most administrators are just survivors. It's easier for them to get behind the paper curtain of the 'Three Bs'—the board, the budget and the bull."

Enochs has an almost macho sense of what leadership means. He quotes Albert Camus: "Groups are always more immoral than individuals." He quotes Ralph Waldo Emerson: "A hero is no braver than an ordinary man, but he is brave five minutes longer." And he likes James McGregor Burns's distinction between "transactional" and "transformational" leadership—the difference between being a competent custodian and the more lofty undertaking of attempting fundamental changes, even in hard times. He sees effective school leadership as an "act of elevation, the elevation of standards, performance, and satisfaction." He says it has much more to do with a kind of "mental toughness" than all the tenets of "crisis management, conflict resolution, and shared decision-making." But when he looks closely at his colleagues, he sees a profession afflicted by "shame-faced defeatism," preoccupied more by public relations and pressure groups than what's beneficial for children. He sees mere managers, not leaders—a group of "shell-shocked GIs counting up their points for discharge." And that, Enochs is convinced, is at the heart of the problems of the public schools.

* * *

Jim Enochs represents a certain kind of teacher, principal, and administrator encountered repeatedly during this nationwide search for elementary schools and programs making the grade in urban America. It seems that where kids are learning—particularly in the worst of social circumstances—there is an adult who has decided to lay himself on the line. Leaders make schools work. Those who refuse to allow the increasing bureaucratization of public school systems to encroach upon the relationship between students and their teachers. Those who will not accept excuses, who are not afraid to look for answers. Those who are not merely satisfied with stroking the system but are striving purposefully to recharge it.

This country's major urban school systems—slow-moving and burdened—may well be beyond the powers of one man or woman, but it is clear that any single elementary school can be turned around with the right combination of leadership, instructional effort, and time. If nothing else, the successful schools profiled in this book provide much hope on that score. This is not to imply that the task is easy, that success can simply be mandated from on high. Schools are not simple organizations whose elements can always be manipulated at will. They sit at the center of a great number of competing forces, and a great number of people are party to the enterprise. Of all public endeavors, education is the most vulnerable to human and organizational failings—and the most unresponsive to public policy. Nonetheless, the path to creating successful schools is well-marked, clearly dependent on these critical factors:

Principals

Schools are "street-level bureaucracies." To use an analogy, a police chief can set policy as to how his officers should treat citizens, but the department's real policies are made every minute of the day by each officer as he makes decisions on the street. So with schools: Firm districtwide policies are necessary, but they don't mean a thing unless some way is found to control what happens between teachers and students once the classroom doors are closed. That is the main role of school principals. And so they, more than anyone else, determine the educational fate of their students.

But school systems seem to select, evaluate, reward, and retain principals on every basis but their key function: instructional leadership. Most principals simply lack the background and training to recognize and foster good teaching; they usually have not risen to their positions because they possess expertise in beginning reading, the most critical task of elementary schools. They have their eye on the mandates of the bureaucracy, rather than on the academic needs of their students and teachers. This is encouraged by the structure of large public school systems: The higher educators advance, the farther they get away from the classroom. It is enforced by the relatively small degree of autonomy accorded principals by their administrative superiors: They are expected to be mere managers, and most have settled for that. "Being caught up in the demands of the district office and the routines of management, most of which could be done better and less expensively by someone else, the principal has no time for the development of programs and people within the school," John Goodlad, dean of the Graduate School of Education at the University of California, Los Angeles, wrote in the January, 1979 issue of *Phi Delta Kappan* magazine. "This . . . conspires with the status elements of the job to cause principals to play their cards close to their chests, making their lonely jobs even lonelier."

Good principals, by contrast, tend to rock the boat. They exude watchfulness—over everyone and everything within their purview. They foresake the desire to be loved for the hard task of monitoring students' progress. They set achievement goals for their students, and they judge themselves and their teachers by these objectives. They plan the best uses of the resources at their disposal, however meager. And they are willing to be held accountable for the results of these decisions. Of the strength and dedication it takes to be an effective principal, Goodlad noted, "Almost invariably, too, the [successful] principal is a person with a strong sense of personal worth and potency, one who takes positions on issues and is not regarded as a pawn of the superintendent or of strong individuals or groups within the community."

There is no more critical decision in public education than the employment of a principal. "If you want to turn things around," said Gilbert Austin, a University of Maryland researcher, "choose a principal with an instructional background and a sense of purpose, establish student performance goals and leave him there for five years. Let him know his job depends on how he meets these goals."

Belief

Belief that students can learn—that the job can be done well—is the foundation of true accountability. It is, however, a rare attitude among educators. Said Dennis Gray, associate director of the Council for Basic Education: "The thing about 'all children can learn' is that it turns out to be one of those truisms that a lot of people don't believe. A lot of teachers don't believe it; the disbelief is so pervasive that a lot of parents don't believe it when it comes to their own children. There are all kinds of excuses floating around: 'What do you expect, these children can't even speak English.' . . . 'Black kids can't learn as well as white.' . . . 'The poor can't learn as well as the rich.' "

Instead of assuming that kids can learn and searching for the most effective ways to teach, many educators appear to act like consulting physicians who have been brought in to advise dispassionately on a very difficult, perhaps hopeless case. They cloak their impotency in the trappings of professionalism and shield it from the public by a thick armor of jargon. Image management has replaced results, with their journals advising them on the best way to bring the "good news" of public education to the forefront. As one Cincinnati principal put it in 1979: "About ten years ago, we gave up worrying about what we did with kids and started concentrating on what we say we do." The reason for this, of course, is that it is far easier to believe that children can't really learn, for then it follows closely that educators can't be held to any strict performance standards. "For all the current rhetoric about test scores and accountability," said Fritz Mulhauser of the National Institute of Education, "when did a school ever go out of business for not doing well by its students?" And one might also ask: When was the last time a public educator—particularly an administrator—lost his job for that same reason?

Beliefs, in a society with a long history of racism and classism, are hard to alter. But a firm tenet of education is, "What you expect, you get." And so as Ron Edmonds, assistant chancellor of the New York City schools, suggests, the first step to reforming public schools is to repudiate the deep-seated notion that certain children can't learn as well as others. On this issue, the adults at schools that work seem to have reached a consensus in favor of their students, enabling everyone to focus on the hard matter of instruction. These schools possess an ethos, a climate of high standards and high expectations. If they are exceptional in that they serve low-income children well, their secret is that they have the same achievement standards and goals as schools in middle-class areas and are intolerant of excuses, however sophisticated.

Instruction

In all the debate over the problems afflicting the public schools, instruction—what happens when the teacher closes the classroom door—is seldom mentioned. "The function of education is to teach kids," said Wesley Becker, co-developer of DISTAR, "but most educators prefer to pay attention to dollars and adult interactions." A good example of this misplaced emphasis is a 1979 report on the problems of the Cincinnati Public Schools, written by Hendrik Gideonse, dean of the University of Cincinnati's College of Education and Home Economics. Gideonse discusses in great detail the school system's financial problems, its legal problems, and its public relations problems. But not one section of his 25-page report deals with the problem of instruction. The message is clear: Instruction is not a critical issue; it doesn't make much difference what's done in the classroom.

But this is sheer blindness; at every school the quality of instruction is the most critical issue, what makes the most difference. And not recognizing this verges on outright deception, for both surveying educational research and observing classrooms in successful schools across the country lead to the same, overriding conclusion: Student achievement results from time spent directly and efficiently on teaching academic skills in a highly structured, teacher-controlled environment. What works is increasing students' "academic engaged time." A strong academic focus works. Systematic phonics works. So do direct instruction techniques. So does restoring the primary responsibility for students' achievement to their regular classroom teachers. All this is why such seemingly regimented instructional programs as the mastery learning lessons in Chicago and DISTAR produce results: They control the details of what happens between students and teachers so that many of these effective processes take place.

The advocates of less-structured, "open" education, of indirectly relevant classroom exercises based on the idea of "learning how to learn," of "humanistic" programs focusing on the children's individual sense of self-worth—all would protest vehemently against this conclusion. This is narrow, mechanistic, oppressive, unappreciative of children's different styles of learning, joyless, they'd say. "In education, if you say let's teach reading carefully, you're labeled a reactionary," said DISTAR designer Siegfried Engelmann, who's been the target of such charges for years. "To be liberal in education is to ignore teaching in favor of a bunch of slogans like, 'Pay attention to the whole child.'" But there is no greater enslavement of the "whole child" than not teaching him how to read well; and the hard evidence on this score runs overwhelmingly against the proponents of "open" education. Ironically, there also is good evidence that the classrooms in which children feel best about themselves are not those in which "affective" programs take precedence, but those in which children are achieving—the more structured and controlled environments.

None of this represents a great discovery, the unraveling of a deep mystery; it is available to any layman with the time and inclination to pursue the question. But at the same time, it has been largely ignored by many educators, by a profession, in Goodlad's words, "relatively weak . . . badly divided within itself and not yet embodying the core of professional values and knowledge required to resist fads, special interest groups, and—perhaps most serious of all—funding influences." Public education is a $130-billion-a-year industry, crippled absurdly by the pernicious tendency to judge the merits of instructional programs according to their political or philosophical currency, rather than their actual results. "There is almost no [research] literature which suggests that the impact of a program has an effect on policy, on even whether it's allowed to stay in place," said Dick Jung, research director of the National Advisory Council on the Education of Disadvantaged Children. "Policy decisions in education are just not made that rationally."

So justifying failure becomes a way of life in the public schools. Bad ideas—ones that clearly don't work for large numbers of children—gain remarkable credibility as they are allowed to linger. And good ideas—even ones that produce dramatic results with children resistant to most other efforts—spawn resentment and fear. So publishers walk away with profits from pushing programs that have never been subjected to honest tests, never have been shown to work. Systematic phonics—regarded as the superior approach to beginning reading for at least a decade—remains far from widely used. And $3.5 billion a year flows from

Washington, D.C., to compensatory education programs in some 90 percent of the school districts in the country without one cent of this money contingent on the public schools taking responsibility for the achievement of the six million children in these programs.

So mere effort, if even that, is allowed to be substituted for results, and nary a negative word is supposed to be uttered—except about children's abilities to learn. More labels to describe students' deficiencies are created. The shamefully low standard of three-quarters of a year gain on achievement tests for every year in school becomes the accepted norm, all that can be expected. Programs that patently discriminate against children who do not receive much education in school skills at home—such as "discovery-oriented" classrooms—are upheld as wisdom. The achievement gap grows wider with each passing year; the answers are sought everywhere but in the classroom, in the process of teaching. And nothing changes.

Teachers

Every school system in the country is faced with the problem of ill-trained, incompetent teachers. Horror stories abound in this respect. But they are not just hollow tales: When the first competency tests were given to teachers in the late 1970s in Dallas, Houston, Mobile, and the state of Georgia, up to half the would-be teachers failed to score as well in basic academic skills as the average high-school junior. "It's not so much that we have so few good teachers," said George Weber, a long-time education researcher and critic. "It's a wonder that we have any at all."

There are two culprits here. One is the rapidly declining economic and social status of teaching; as a profession, it is attracting what Samuel Halperin, director of the Institute for Educational Leadership, aptly calls "the leftovers," those neither prepared for nor motivated by the challenges and rewards of the private sector. Compounding this is the caliber of training offered at schools of education, where standards have declined along with their market. Many are still promoting "open" education theories from the 1960s, and few are adequately exposing their students to the realities of urban public school classrooms. "Teachers come out of school without any kind of background or experience to teach beginning reading at the elementary level," said Jim Enochs. "There's no sense in waiting for the colleges to reform." He is right, but that should not imply the problem is insolvable.

The alternatives, in fact, are many. Stricter accountability measures, including competency screening tests and annual evaluations tied to students' performance, are a beginning. They are not likely to be accepted by teachers nor will they work unless they are tied to similar standards for principals and administrators and put into effect only after extensive retraining. Most "in-service" training is a sham, little more than one-shot sessions which have a minimal effect on what happens in the classroom. By contrast, programs that work, such as mastery learning and DISTAR, demand that many hours be spent on learning specific, effective teaching behaviors and then require that these be used in the classroom. "Everyone says, 'Oh, teachers will never accept accountability,' " said Engelmann. "But all they really want is for someone to demonstrate to them that it can be done, that they will be provided with the tools to do the job. That's the point, of course, when administrators back down."

Instituting a new system of rewards for teachers is another possibility. The most commonly proposed method is "combat pay," additional money for those who choose to teach in impoverished settings. But this is a negative concept and does not insure that the best teachers end up in classrooms where they are needed the most. Engelmann has proposed a positive way of reversing the system of rewards that would put the most effective teachers with high concentrations of low-achieving students. Right now experienced teachers in urban public school systems are rewarded not so much by extra money as the eventual opportunity to transfer to white, middle-class enclaves, where they can work with high achievers; new, inexperienced teachers—and the incompetents—often are shuttled downtown. Under Engelmann's proposal, all beginning teachers first would be put in classes with high-achieving children, and they'd be paid less than the average salary. If their students show standard gains for two years in a row, he'd let them work with average students, raising their pay to the average level. If they show results with these kids for two years, then, and only then, would he let them teach low achievers, with whom they would make more than the average salary. Incidentally, under this setup, he wouldn't allow anyone to become a supervisor unless he had successfully taught high-risk children. And he'd employ "educational monitors," quality-control inspectors independent of school system bureaucracies, to document and report ineffective teaching. For the school board truly interested in teaching all children, these monitors would be child advocates.

Finally, there is the little-used alternative of firing teachers. Getting rid of incompetent teachers in heavily unionized, large school systems would seem to be next to impossible; a relative handful are told to leave each year in most cities—usually only when there is evidence that they have committed an immoral or illegal act. To a great extent, so few are fired not because the teacher unions' lawyers are so much better than the school systems', but because teachers' instructional responsibilities are not well-defined, standards are set abysmally low, and principals are not encouraged to do anything about bad teaching. It comes back to the issue of making principals take responsibility for the instruction at their schools. As it stands, good principals do try to get rid of incompetent teachers and sometimes succeed, chiefly by putting enough pressure on to get them to quit. By the same token, these principals tend to attract and retain good teachers not because they have more money to offer or because the children at their schools are any easier to educate, but because they find ways to support good teaching. As the teachers in their schools invariably report: "He's a good principal because he makes it possible for us to do our jobs—he lets us teach." On the other hand, ask competent teachers why they quit the public schools, and they usually say, "I got tired of working for fools, of not having any support."

Resources

Perhaps the favorite excuse of educators is that the job can't be done without the funds. Certainly, the public schools in many urban areas are under-funded, particularly where the primary means of financial support remains local property taxes. However, this is nothing more than a red herring when it comes to explaining the success or failure of schools. What counts is not how much schools have, but what they do with what they have.

Witness the 20,000-pupil East St. Louis, Illinois, schools—a system serving a decaying town without industry and with a hard-to-shake reputation for corrupt government, a system so impoverished that no one will buy its bonds voted years ago. East St. Louis students—almost all black, more than 70 percent from welfare families—leave the sixth grade reading nearly at normal grade level according to standardized tests, a record that few large school systems can match.

Or take note of a 1976 University of Missouri study of 17 Kansas City elementaries which received $25 million in special local, state, and federal assistance (beyond normal per-pupil support) to improve the education of low-income students between 1965 and 1975. In that ten-year period, achievement levels at these schools did not improve. The same result was found in a 1977 Rand Corporation study of 11 impoverished New York City elementaries which received some $40 million in federal funds over four years.

Small class sizes, high teacher salaries, new buildings, or good equipment don't necessarily mean students will receive an education, although all these conditions may be preferable in themselves. Pouring additional money into schools is not likely to make much of a difference in student achievement unless the extra resources are accompanied by more fundamental changes in the schools' instructional programs and general climate. Time and people are the only true resources that schools possess; to the extent that school-level leadership mobilizes and focuses these resources efficiently on firm instructional goals, achievement follows. "There's no magic answer," said Tom Tomlinson of the National Institute of Education. "There's only good teaching and hard work, which implies time. If kids' abilities are low, then you have to work harder, use time more efficiently, to make up for that. The schools that insist that kids do that—the ones that let teachers teach—produce better outcomes. Typically, schools are so poorly managed as to not allow children to learn; they squander people and time. Good schools are structured so there is a minimum of outside distractions and so children spend more time on the learning process." This applies to all schools, not just those in low-income areas. Few schools are running at full blast. The failings of middle-class schools, however, are not so readily obvious because their students tend to receive more education in the skills demanded by school in their homes.

The essential question, then, is how a productive instructional focus is developed.

In this respect, much is made of the potential power of parents. Ron Edmonds, for instance, believes that educational equity will not come about until low-income parents gain full political power. He, therefore, calls parents' involvement in politics "the greatest instrument of instructional reform extant." This is an appealing argument, but, to a certain extent, it is circular, for poverty and the lack of political power are inseparable components of the same condition. Moreover, this search for effective schools in low-income urban areas did not uncover a single instance where parents had been a critical factor in shaping a successful school. And many observers believe this is indicative of the reality of public education, that parents—particularly those in low-income areas—are simply no match for educators. "Parents are getting raped by the schools and don't even know it," said Engelmann. "I pity them. They have no say whatsoever."

This may seem to be an overstatement, but even those working for national organizations dedicated to increasing parent participation in public education find no quarrel with it in reference to impoverished communities. "Nationwide, I don't see any reason for euphoria about the power of parents in low-income areas," said Carl Marburger, senior associate at the National Council for Citizens in Education. He added that he, too, couldn't cite an example of a school where low-income parents had tackled successfully the issue of school quality. "It can happen," he said, "but it's darn tough if you're talking about meaningful issues, governance issues—not just the color of the bunting hanging in the school's auditorium. The roadblocks are tremendous, most particularly the fortress mentality of school administrators."

The impotency of Parent Advisory Councils, mandated as part of the federal Title I program for low-achieving, low-income students, is illustrative. The great majority of these councils do nothing but carry out administrative errands. Their unstated, but actual function usually is to serve as buffers, insulating the schools from the public. In the rural South, parent councils are still struggling to achieve recognition, to gain access to basic information about their children's schools. Even with recognition, parents' groups usually find themselves totally dependent on the suspect evaluations provided by school officials. "It requires a great deal of sophistication," said Hayes Mizell, chairman of the National Advisory Council on Education of Disadvantaged Children (the national Title I parents' organization) and a former Columbia, South Carolina, school board member. "School boards have the same problems as parent councils—believe it or not. They're supposed to be so powerful, yet they're often manipulated by school administrators. For board members, it's very hard to not let yourself be defined—have your power limited—by the very professionals who are supposed to be working for you. You've got to be willing to say no, to ask hard questions and to demand that they be accountable for the answers."

In addition to the increasingly entrenched and self-serving power of their own administrative staffs, school boards also have lost authority over educational matters to the courts, to state and federal government agencies, and to teachers' unions. Educational critic Paul Copperman has documented the rise of this "enormous centralization of authority" through the 1960s and 1970s. And he views it as having greatly hampered the power of local communities to exert educational leadership through their school boards at a time of social flux when this kind of authority was most needed. Even so, Copperman believes that the potential remains great for boards willing to become more than rubber stamps. "There has to be a politicization of the educational process in the community," he said in an April 1980 address to the Education Writers Association. "The school board has to talk with a louder voice and has to seize back some of the authority, some of that power over educational policy. School boards have to set policy in curriculum, personnel, discipline and evaluation. . . . They have to be educational vehicles to educate their own communities in this kind of vision of effective schooling. . . ."

But it is the rare school board that has been inclined and able to use its political power to forge such educational leadership in its schools. Like less-powerful parent organizations, they more often deal only with the "color of the bunting hanging in the school's auditorium." The deck seems to be stacked heavily in favor of those administering the operations of school systems, possibly the only group within urban public education that has a vested interest in maintaining the status quo.

This is a depressing conclusion, tempered only by the examples set by an unusual group of dedicated educators who have not strayed too far from the classroom and who have refused to give up on the frustrating challenges facing the public schools. The story of exceptional schools, for now, appears to be the story of exceptional people, of leaders, of adults who are taking responsibility for their students' education, who are making a difference in children's lives.

It is the story of principals like Carol Russo, who will not allow the devastation of the South Bronx to creep into her school building; teachers like Walter Thompson at the May School in Chicago, who is convinced there isn't that much difference in ability among children; program designers like Siegfried Engelmann and Michael Katims, who have taken the hard route of analyzing how to teach all children; and administrators like Alice Blair on the south side of Chicago, who has set out to prove that "these kids can learn."

They are inspiring, a source of hope for the future of urban public education. They remain minute points of brilliance in a vast, intolerably bleak field.